THE UNIFICATION OF GERMANY

or

THE ANATOMY OF A PEACEFUL REVOLUTION

by

Peter Neckermann

EAST EUROPEAN MONOGRAPHS, BOULDER
DISTRIBUTED BY COLUMBIA UNIVERSITY PRESS, NEW YORK

1991

EAST EUROPEAN MONOGRAPHS, NO. CCCIII

for Jutta

Contents

A LIST OF THE MAIN GERMAN PARTIES AND THEIR COMMON ABBREVIATIONS

1. West German Parties

Christlich–Demokratische Union – Christian Demoratic Party – CDU

Christlich–Soziale Union – Christian–Social Party – CSU

CDU/CSU – These sister parties (the CSU exists only in Bavaria, the CDU in the other parts of West Germany) together form a bourgeois catchall party whose actions are anchored in conservative beliefs and in the Christian social ethics.

Die Gruenen – The Greens is a party that comprises the environmentalists, the peace movement, feminist groups, and others who feel that our civilization has estranged the people from the basic values of life.

Freie Demokratische Partei – Free Democratic Party – F.D.P. It is the party of European liberalism. Its objective is to defend the individual against the encroachment of the state, of unions, of bureaucracy, and of any other powerful but anonymous organization.

Die Sozialdemokratische Partei Deutschlands – Social–Democratic Party of Germany – SPD – This left–leaning catchall party is committed to democracy and social equality.

2. East German Parties

Christlich–Demokratische Union – Christian Democratic Party – CDU (now merged with its West German counterpart)

Deutsche Soziale Union – German Social Union – DSU – This small center/right party is based on the Christian social ethic.

Demokratische Bauernpartei Deutschlands – Democratic Peasant Party of Germany – DBD – This small party represents the interests of the farm community.

Freie Demokratische Partei – Free Democratic Party – F.D.P. – (now merged with its West German counterpart)

Gruene Partei – Green Party – It is an environmentalist party.

Neues Forum – New Forum – It was the roof organization of the 1989 emerging discussion and protest groups that organized the demonstrations which led to the downfall of the communist regime. Now it is a small center/left party.

Partei des Demokratischen Sozialismus – Party of Democratic Socialism – PDS – This successor of the communist party in East Germany is now committed to the realization of a democratic–socialist state.

Sozialdemokratische Partei Deutschlands – Social–Democratic Party of Germany – SPD (now merged with its West German counterpart)

FOREWORD

In the autumn of 1987, President Ronald Reagan visited Berlin and was greeted by hostile demonstrations. In a memorable speech, he demanded the removal of the Berlin Wall and unification of Germany. At that time, I, like most other people, believed that his words were wishful thinking. I did not see how at any time soon, Western ideology could triumph over communism or how a Soviet leader would give up Eastern Europe without being forced to do so by war. Usually empires do not wither away; they are destroyed when their vitality is gone and bureaucratic stagnation has set in.

When Reagan visited Berlin for a second time in 1990, he was welcomed as a hero. He walked through the Brandenburg Gate from one part of the united city into the other. In the short period of time between Reagan's two visits, Gorbachev's reform movement had changed the international political environment, the East German people had had a peaceful revolution, and through international and internal negotiations West Germany's Chancellor Kohl had achieved the unification of Germany. When the "Treaty on the Final Settlement With Respect to Germany" was finally presented to the Conference on Security and Cooperation in Europe in New York on October 1, 1990, the postwar period came to an end.

The events in 1989 and 1990 were so remarkable that I felt obligated to write them down while they were fresh in my memory. I did not want hindsight to disturb my original observations and thoughts. I am deeply indebted to Drs. Jan and Arthur Adams whose encouragement and guidance led to the completion of this manuscript. Dr. Thomas Minnick deserves great praise for the final form of the essay. Further thanks goes to Vivian Beatel who sacrificed many hours to write and rewrite the manuscript. Much admiration goes to my wife, Jutta, for her patience and encouragement at the right moments.

I hope that this essay will contribute to the memory of great political leaders and East German people who had the courage to act and thus accomplish a life in freedom and prosperity for many who had suffered under communist oppression.

Peter Neckermann
Columbus, Ohio
March 1991

INTRODUCTION

One major result of the last world war was the division of the world into a Soviet hemisphere ruled by communism and a U.S. hemisphere where democracy flourished. In Europe the border between these zones, the "iron curtain," ran through Germany, dividing the country into a larger Western and a smaller Eastern part. Immediately after the war, German politicians tried to unite these parts but failed. Thus, two separate states emerged on Germany's soil. One, West Germany, became a democracy, the European outpost of the Western world. The other, East Germany, became a communist state, the border of the Soviet empire toward the West. Over the years, the Germans and their politicians realized that a peaceful unification of these two states would become possible only when the separation of the world into two competing hemispheres would come to an end and when the iron curtain would lose its importance.

Until 1989, most people believed that the competition between the U. S. and the Soviet Union, the superpowers, would not wane in the twentieth century, so no one expected that a chance for a peaceful unification would arise. Since Western citizens and politicians alike agreed that the border of the Soviet empire should not be altered by force, one precondition for an eventual unification of Germany was established. The superpower competition had to abate before unification could become a feasible political proposition.

Since war was not supposed to change the border of the Soviet zone of influence in Europe, the willingness to lower or abolish the iron curtain had to come from within the Soviet Union. The commmunist system, by 1985, was petrified. That a man committed to revitalizing it by breaking up its incrustations could rise to the top is a miracle. Mikhail Gorbachev deserves admiration for his willingness to unleash forces of change without knowing the outcome of the experiment. He started an economic and political reform process from the top downward, a process which found fertile soil ready to absorb

the message for change in some places but not everywhere. The Soviet people's aspirations had been crushed so often in the past that
initially they were not sure whether they should accept his advances
or not. Citizens in the East European satellites of the Soviet Union
remembered when they had dared to revolt against communist rule:
1953 in East Berlin, 1956 in Budapest, 1968 in Prague. Each time,
the Red Army had crushed their revolts and fortified the rule of the
communist cliques. The Brezhnev doctrine of "Once a communist
country, ever a communist country" was accepted political currency
in both East and West.

Yet, under the seemingly stable and unchallenged communist
rule, the desire for freedom and self–determination never totally died.
It even gained strength in recent years and pierced the surface in the
shipyards of Gdansk. Shipyard workers created their own union, "Solidarity," and challenged the claim of the communist party to be the
sole legitimate representative of the people. At this critical moment,
people in the East and West waited, full of anxiety, to see whether
Gorbachev would follow the example of his predecessors. Gorbachev
accepted the results of his policies of *glasnost* and *perestroika* and
allowed the breakup of the monolithic communist rule. He did not
allow the Red Army to crush the rebellion in Gdansk. Did Gorbachev
know that his policies would lead to the liberation of Eastern Europe
from communism? We know only that he made the vital decision not
to use force to defend the petrified communist system which ruled
Eastern Europe and the Soviet Union.

His decision not to use force in defense of the East European
regimes changed the global political equation. A new flexibility entered European politics and the superpower relations. Suddenly, the
iron curtain seemed to lose some of its rigidity. The decision to pro-
mote reforms, even if they meant the end of the communist monopoly
on power, opened up an opportunity for changes in the global and European political landscape. Some people began to envision that the
final step in a long process of convergence between East and West
would be the unification of Germany.

Without the threat of outside intervention, the East European
people got the chance to take their fate into their own hands. Suddenly, the East Europeans confronted only their own governments,
each with its own apparatus of suppression. The East Europeans
sensed that they had a chance to alter their living conditions and
governments if they firmly requested Gorbachev's reform program

to be realized in their respective countries. These requests, voiced in demonstrations, grew into genuine revolutions that shattered the communist rule.

The East Germans, whose country was an important part of the Soviet security zone in Europe, were not the first to stand up against their communist government. But when in 1989, the East German people started to demonstrate and later revolted against their oppressors, their revolution became the second ingredient or precondition for the unification of Germany in 1990.

The third ingredient necessary for successful unification was the availability of a determined and astute West German leader willing to bet his political future on the success or failure of the immediate unification process. In the early hours of the demonstrations, the East German people demanded participation in government and free travel to the West. Later, they widened their demands to include the ouster of the communist regime, the demise of the East German state, and the unification with West Germany. Now, international political questions of great sensitivity came into play, questions which could not be resolved by the East German people alone. An astute political leader with an international reputation and influence was necessary to translate the people's demands into discussions and actions at the international political level. Such a leader was available in Helmut Kohl, chancellor of West Germany. Supported by his foreign minister, Hans–Dietrich Genscher, Kohl realized the uniqueness of the situation and seized it with great political savvy. Guided by great determination and knowledge of when to make the right moves, Kohl successfully united Germany in 1990, forty–five years after World War II had torn the country apart.

I believe that the unification would not have happened if, for example, Oskar Lafontaine, the socialist challenger for the West German chancellorship, had been leading West Germany at that point in time. For in order to achieve the unification of Germany, three things had to come together. First, the superpower competition had to abate, and the iron curtain had to became obsolete. Second, East German people had to want not only a reform of their government but also a dissolution of their country and a unification with West Germany. Finally, a statesman capable of seizing the opportunity had to be present with the skill to tie together a new web of international, European, and German relations.

Tempo was an important element of this political change. The events unfolded with such speed between May of 1989 and October of 1990 that the politicians involved came close to exhaustion. Some mainly from the opposition, again and again demanded a slower speed and would have liked to see unification delayed to 1991. With hind-sight, one sees that the window of opportunity was open for only a very limited period of time. Astute observers of East–West relations convincingly argue that if it had not been achieved in October of 1990, unification would not be possible today.

In the following essay, I hope to convince the reader that the above thesis correctly claims that three preconditions were needed for the successful unification of Germany. The international situation had to change, the East German people had to stand up not only against their government but for unification, and a prominent West German leader had to be available to translate the people's demands into international political discussions, actions, and agreements.

I. THE POLITICAL SITUATION IN SPRING OF 1989

In the spring of 1989, Gorbachev's program to reform the economic and, if necessary, the political structures had a mixed reception in East European capitals.[1] Most communist regimes hesitated, for they feared that the reform process might slip out of their hands and eventually sweep them away. But some regimes, better prepared than others, were more open to change.

The most progressive regime was in Budapest.[2] Since the early eighties, the Hungarian communists had tried to liberalize their economy in small incremental steps. Individuals were encouraged to start up small businesses, particularly in the service industry, and contacts to the West were nursed. The communist officials openly admitted that to move their economy out of stagnation and into a period of growth, they would need to increase trade and information exchanges with the West. In 1988, this economic opening forced adjustments on the political system. Independent political organizations began to emerge. The communist party could have prevented them but did not do so. Some of these associations developed into political parties and announced their intention to compete for legislative seats in the 1990 parliamentary elections. The Hungarian experiment, hotly debated in the East and West, was eventually legitimized by Gorbachev's reform movement.

In Poland, the shipyard workers of Gdansk had taken their fate in their own hands and had created their own union, "Solidarity," which challenged the claim of the communist party to be the sole legitimate representative of the people.[3] Solidarity survived martial law and by 1989 had broken the communist monopoly of power in Poland.

In other East European capitals—East Berlin, Prague, Bucharest, and Sofia—the communists were firmly in control. They resisted Gorbachev's request and did not start a reform process. They argued repeatedly that a reform process would only undermine their political dominance and the stability of their countries and thus of the Soviet hemisphere. On the last point they were correct, although nobody could have known that weakening the economic command structure would immdiately lead to a breakdown of the communist regimes.[4]

The Honecker regime in East Germamy openly opposed Gorbachev's reform movement. Erich Honecker, the president of East Germany, used every opportunity to criticize Moscow and to compare the Soviet situation with the stability of his regime and the economic progress it had made.[5] Though East Germany was the forward bastion of the Soviet empire, the relationship between Moscow and East Berlin cooled considerably. Honecker was arguably the most prominent of the hard-liners in Eastern Europe; and most observers believed that he and his regime had the wherewithal to sustain themselves in power, despite Moscow's disapproval. The East Germans showed no signs of unrest; the political situation was calm in the spring of 1989.

At the superpower level, some carefully orchestrated movements could be detected.[6] Already at the Reykjavik summit meeting in December of 1989, Gorbachev had suggested sweeping changes in the relations between the two superpowers. But these suggestions were too sweeping and too vague to elicit a positive response from the Reagan administration. Nevertheless, the cold war atmosphere had gradually given way to a more conciliatory tone. The mutual sense of a growing rapprochement found its public expression in the first summit meeting between Bush and Gorbachev in Malta in December of 1989. Despite the stormy weather in Malta, the meeting became a pathbreaking success. Bush and Gorbachev agreed in principle that the superpower competition had to end and that both powers needed to find new patterns of cooperation in a world they no longer tightly controlled. Americans reasonably concluded from Gorbachev's remarks that the opportunity existed for ending the division of Europe in exchange for America's support of the communist reform movement. Bush realized that a historic chance was presented to him, and he in turn promised economic support and abstention from any political action that might destabilize the Soviet Union.

But Moscow and Washington were unequal partners at the Malta summit. Moscow was in the process of losing control and influence over Eastern Europe, while the partnership of the U. S. with Western Europe was *not* at stake. Moscow's control over its hemisphere rested primarily on a common ideology and its military supremacy.[7] But the ideology was rapidly losing its luster, and the military instrument could hardly be used to coerce people into higher productivity. The U .S.–European partnership rested on very different pillars—a common heritage of freedom and individualism which promised that this partnership would last, even if the U. S. were no longer the dominant force.[8]

The political situation within Europe and between the superpowers had become more fluid than most people and political leaders realized in the spring of 1989. Gorbachev's reform movement had undermined the stability and even the legality of the communist regimes in Eastern Europe. The superpower relationship had emerged out of the cold war into a new era of cooperation. What nobody fully realized was the extent to which people in Eastern Europe were ready to take their fate into their own hands. The speed of change accelerated in the spring of 1989. In a matter of months, the will of the people overcame the resistance of their entrenched governments to Gorbachev's reforms. By the end of summer, East Germans, Hungarians, and Czechoslovakians went into the streets and wrested the power out of communist hands. These demonstrations turned into revolutions. In other East European countries such as Romania and Bulgaria, those developments occurred later. But all of them brought about the demise of the hated communist regimes. About a year later, the nations of Eastern Europe had new governments and for all intents and purposes had moved out of the Soviet orbit.

II. FROM COMMUNISM TO PLURALISM IN EAST GERMANY

A. The Reform Movement in September and October of 1989

The Honecker regime in East Germany resisted Gorbachev's requests for reforms. Honecker argued until his ouster that the economic and political successes of his regime made reforms unnecessary. Many East Germans disagreed. They either left the country at the first possible opportunity or spontaneously gathered in groups and circles, requesting political and economic changes. The reform movememt in East Germany was initiated by the people in spite of the firm opposition of the regime. This popular movement accomplished what most observers believed was impossible.

Honecker's regime was based on a disciplined party, an efficient bureaucracy, and a well–informed secret police (Stasi). It seemed to be firmly in control in the summer of 1989. East Germany, the most successful communist country of the Eastern Bloc, had enjoyed political stability since the aborted coup in 1953. The living standard was higher than in any other communist country. Erich Honecker even believed that East Germany was on the verge of becoming the "silicon valley" of the East Bloc because Robotron, the state–owned electronic concern, had just developed a four megabyte chip.

East German government officials, Honecker included, made it clear by speeches and actions that they would not implement changes that could endanger the communist party's position of leadership, as had occurred in Poland and Hungary. The East German people believed what their government said. Because they were convinced that their government would never change, that the communist rule would continue, a sense of hopelessness spread. This explains why many vacationing East Germans used the opportunity of the opening of the Hungarian border to flee via Austria to West Germany. When they left behind family and friends, they had to believe that they would not be able to see them again for many years to come. East Germany branded them as deserters and would have jailed them, had they dared to return. To them West Germany, where consumer goods were abundantly available, was a strange country with different work habits and lifestyles. The citizens who turned their backs on East Germany included many young workers with good jobs and a secure future. But they gave this up, preferring an uncertain future in freedom.

In most of the Eastern Bloc, travel to the West was severely restricted. The mutual assistance treaty of 1969 obligated all communist countries to capture emigrants who tried to cross the iron curtain and to return them to their home country for punishment and prison. But in 1989 the situation was different in Hungary, which used Gorbachev's reforms to speed up its own opening toward the West. The Hungarian leadership hoped for Western support for their economic reforms and knew that eventually the iron curtain had to be transformed into an ordinary border, separating independent but not hostile countries. Hungary's Foreign Minister, Gyula Horn, made the decision to take the first step in August of 1989.[1] He informed Bonn and later East Berlin that he would no longer honor the 1969 assistance treaty—that is, he would not return refugees to East Germany. Horn later reported the "arrogant behavior" of his East German counterpart when he brought up the problem of refugees, indicating how deeply divided the Eastern Bloc actually was at this point in time. When it became known that Hungary would not return refugees to East Germany and rumors started that the border to Austria would be opened, 6,000 East Germans gathered at the West German embassy in Budapest and many more camped along the Hungarian/Austrian border.[2] On September 10, 1989, the Hungarian border was opened. The iron curtain that had sealed off the communist world from the West for forty-four years developed a major hole.

Why was it that the East Germans, not the Hungarians, seized this opportunity and fled into the West? The simplest answer is that the East Germans had German passports and the Hungarians did not. The German Basic Law postulates that there is only one German nation. Therefore, all Germans, whether they lived in East or West Germany, had a German passport and were theoretically free to live in the state they preferred. East Germany never stopped its efforts to get from West Germany the concession that the passports and citizenship of the two states should be independent.[3] If this division had ever been implemented, the "legal right" to escape from the East

German "prison" would not have been available in 1989.

East Germany countered the embarrassing mass flight of its citizens by stopping the issue of visas for Hungary, so East Germans fled to neighboring Czechoslovakia. They left their little Trabants in front of the Nicolei church and sought refuge in the West German embassy. The Czechoslovakian authorities did not know how to react. East Germany requested a hard–line approach, but the Czech government had to consider whether Czechoslovakia would ruin its relations with West Germany merely to support communist solidarity. Did communist solidarity necessarily include the physical separation of East and West? The Czechoslovakian government decided to remain neutral and requested that East Berlin should find a solution for the refugee problem.[4]

The East German regime needed to end this embarrassing situation: it was about to celebrate its forty–year state anniversary with President Gorbachev as the guest of honor.[5] Forcing refugees to return to East Germany was out of the question. Letting them stay for a prolonged period in the West German embassy was also no solution because of the aggravating daily media reports. Therefore, the East German authorities, clenching their teeth, acquiesced to the request of West Germany's Foreign Minister Genscher to allow these refugees to go to West Germany. The East Germans asked only that a train be used to carry the refugees through their former homeland to their new destination. The East Germans hoped to humiliate the refugees with this journey, but to the contrary, people gathered everywhere and waved goodbye to this "freedom train."[6]

The atmosphere was tense when Gorbachev came as the guest of honor to the fortieth anniversary of East Germany's statehood. The Honecker regime felt threatened by the exodus of so many of its people. And many of the citizens who stayed were increasingly bold in their request for reforms. During the summer months, in almost every city, small groups had sprung up, discussing and requesting reforms and urging their countrymen to stay and support their demands. Honecker did not dare to oppose them with the full force of his security apparatus. Such actions could have ruined Gorbachev's visit and the reputation of his state just at the time of celebration.

By October 1989, 45,000 East Germans left their homes and belongings behind and fled to West Germany, causing a major blow to Honecker's understanding of the situation in his country and a substantial drain of productive resources. Honecker wanted to convince

Gorbachev of East Germany's need for solidarity from the other communist countries. He wanted the borders sealed off again.

Most of the East German public expected quite a different message from Gorbachev's visit. They hoped for support of their request for reforms. The people demanded change in general, the end of the communist monopoly of power, and the right to travel into the West. Gorbachev was received like a liberator. Wherever he went, crowds gathered to shout "Gorby, Gorby," and Gorbachev did not disappoint them; he disappointed the communist functionaries instead. Publicly and privately, he warned that the communists had to jump on the bandwagon of reform if they wanted to have a chance to remain in power.

At the beginning of October, nobody in East or West Germany thought that a takeover of power from the communists or any kind of unification were realistic possibilities. As late as September 29, 1989, Theo Sommer, the highly respected editor of the magazine *Die Zeit*, wrote that unification had not moved any closer and that, in the interest of peace, East Germany had to remain in the Warsaw Pact.[7] His statement accurately reflected the common sentiment at that time. Most Germans, East and West, still believed that Europe was and would remain divided, and that both Germanies would remain as border states in the opposing camps.

What was planned to be a celebration of harmony unearthed deep divisions instead. The fortieth anniversary of the East German state presented a picture of disharmony between the communist elites in Moscow and East Berlin. Fundamental disagreements about the steps needed for survival surfaced. But even worse for East Germany, Gorbachev's visit cracked the unity, or the *facade* of unity, of the East German Politburo. Horst Sindermann, then number three in the East German hierarchy, described what happened at the celebration on October 7, 1989:

> Gorbachev made a speech that moved me and my colleagues deeply. Without being a know-it-all, he urged us to seize our chance, uttering the now famous phrase, "He who comes late gets punished by life." Honecker did not agree with Gorbachev at all. He went on and on about the successes of the GDR and its four megabyte chip. We were all furious, and the meeting ended in icy silence. After that, we all agreed that Honecker could not remain as secretary-general.[8]

The division in the Politburo became known and had a devastating effect. Some Politburo members advocated a crackdown on the reform movement; others supported the reform movement, either evasively or outright. This deep split prevented the Politburo from taking any decisive actions, and the inactivity of the state gave reform–minded factions more time for generating publicity, for organizing additional discussion groups, and most importantly for staging demonstrations. Those demonstrations had an international audience that weighed heavily on all Politburo decisions. Gorbachev had made it clear that he did not want the image of socialist regimes to be tainted further. This indirectly strengthened the reformers as long as their actions could not be construed to be provocative by international standards.[9] The demonstrations needed to occur without violence and needed to be consistent with Gorbachev's demands.

Leipzig became the center of the reform movement and its demonstrations. Reform groups also emerged in other cities, like Berlin and Dresden, and increasingly caught the attention of the public. In Leipzig, people gathered publicly on Monday nights to discuss their plight. In the fall of 1989, they began marching through the streets carrying burning candles. Soon these vigils developed a life of their own, attracting more and more marchers. On October 2, several hundred people marched. The state security forces arrested some for interrogation. In reaction, several thousand people were expected to participate on October 9. When it became known that the police had decided not to interfere, 70,000 took part in the vigil. A week later, the number had doubled; and on October 23, a crowd of 300,000 people demonstrated for change.[10] The communist regime had lost its opportunity to interfere.

In October of 1989, no organized opposition to the East German communist regime existed; only a general feeling of dissatisfaction and isolation united the people. Some people—among them teachers, clerics, and environmentalists—had started to meet regularly. Churches were the preferred meeting places because they were usually sheltered against intrusion by the security forces. Some groups became popularly known with names like "Democratic Departure," "Citizens' Movement," "Democracy Now," and the "United Left." The "New Forum" became the most permanent group and later the umbrella organization for these protest movements. These groups developed no coherent program but they shared several fundamental objectives:

1. An end to the isolation, with the right to travel freely to the West.

2. A multi-party system.

3. Human rights, meaning an end to the fear that security forces could interrogate and arrest people at will.

4. Changes in the economic system to what was called a "humane socialism." This meant that government would serve first the needs of the people and the environment, not the needs of the state.

The demonstrators neither asked for nor expected the communist leadership to abdicate. They did not contemplate a unification with West Germany. They wanted a share of the power in their own state, and they wanted reforms. In essence, they wanted a socialistic state that would turn its attention to the people. Well into October, the reform movement remained what its name suggested, a popular movement for limited changes in the petrified communist system. The reform wing of the Politburo must have believed that there was still time to follow Gorbachev's advice and to implement some of the people's demands and to survive in power.

B. The Revolution in Winter 1989/1990

The tensions between the Honecker regime and the East German people intensified in October 1989. The communist leaders might have regained the initiative if they had taken up the people's demands and translated them into political actions. But the regime was incapable of such actions; it remained inactive and haunted by demonstrations. In fact, the government's half–hearted promises and timid measures ruined the last bit of goodwill it enjoyed. The opening of the Berlin Wall on November 9, 1989, more accidental than organized, turned into a watershed event that radically changed the people's perceptions. The reform movement turned into a genuine revolution. From then on, a growing number of people no longer wanted merely the reform of the existing system but its downfall and reunification with West Germany.

Erich Honecker abdicated on October 18, 1989. He was followed as president by Egon Krenz, his hard–liner "crown prince." During his four–hour inauguration speech, Krenz promised a "*Wende,*" a term used in West Germany to signal the shift of power from one societal camp to the other. The content, length, and style of his speech were typical for a communist functionary. Krenz was able neither to unite the deeply split Politburo behind him nor to gain any trust among the people. He never recovered the initiative. He and his government continued to be driven by events.

On October 24, there occurred a revolt of modest dimensions. The members of parliament did not vote unanimously for Krenz to become the head of state and chairman of the national defense council. Of the 400 deputies, 26 voted against and another 26 abstained. This was the first time in forty years that opposition was voiced in the East German parliament.

The parliament was not the only institution which showed signs of division. The bureaucracy, the security forces, and even the party itself came under severe strain and showed signs of breaking apart. Some party officials joined the reform movement. Others hesitated to show themselves in public because people approached them and accused them of wrongdoings. Three local officials even committed suicide. Many ordinary party members either burned or sent back their party booklets. Between September 1989 and February 1990, the party shrank from 2.3 million to 890,000 members. The power bases of the regime eroded faster than anybody had believed possible.

Most important, Krenz did not recapture the trust of the East Germans.[1] The exodus from East Germany continued. On the weekend of November 5, more than 10,000 people went via Czechoslovakia into West Germany.[2] Inside East Germany an ever-increasing number of people participated in the demonstrations—more than 500,000 in East Berlin on November 4. People no longer feared the security forces. The Red Army remained invisible, and the police and other security forces were more afraid of the wrath of the masses than they themselves were feared. Krenz tried to appease the masses with a new law that would have allowed some travel to the West. Before it was even discussed in parliament, it was rejected by the public as too restrictive.

A revolutionary atmosphere took hold. The Politburo panicked and lost control of the events on November 9, 1989. According to Krenz's personal account, the leadership was in disarray and unable to make decisions.[3] Some Politburo members, without taking a vote or informing the other members, ordered that selected border crossings to West Berlin should be opened for a limited time. When the media reported this, thousands of East Germans streamed to the Wall and demanded passage. The local authorities didn't dare to stand in their way. Thus the Wall has opened more by accident than by design.

Krenz's account, if correct, demonstrates once more that a dictatorial regime can concentrate and exercise power only as long as it has a true leader and believes in its ideology and itself. It can only survive if those at its pinnacle of power are united and have the guts to defend brutally against public uprisings and other threats. As soon as the regime is weakened by doubts and disunity, the will for brutal defense disappears. Then its power evaporates in a very short period of time. This happened on November 9, 1989, even before the Berlin Wall came down.

After the Berlin Wall opened, millions of East Germans poured into West Berlin and later into West Germany, where they saw with their own eyes how backward their country really was and what freedom really meant.[4] At the same time, stories started to circulate about the good life and privileges the ruling class had reserved for themselves. The media in East and West Germany competed to uncover information about abuses of position and power by the communist leadership. Krenz, himself one of those privileged functionaries, was no longer able to run the government. Hans Modrow was installed as minister–president on November 13, 1989. The former party chief of Dresden, Modrow, was a reformer who had gained some respect from the Dresden population because he kept the security forces at bay during the early demonstrations. Krenz hoped that putting forward a moderate communist as the new minister–president would retain some influence, and with it positions, for hard–liners like himself.

But this was not to be. On December 3, the Politburo and the Central Committee of the party had no option but to resign. Three days later, Krenz stepped down as head of state and made room for the Free Democrat Manfred Gerlach. Two days later the communist party gave up its constitutional leadership role. Gregor Gysi, a 41–year–old lawyer, was elected as the new party leader. The communist party even changed its name from the Socialist Union Party (SED) to the Party of Democratic Socialism (PDS), hoping that new leaders, a new name, and the effort to create a new image would save its political organization and preserve for it an important role in the multi-party system that was slowly emerging.

The demonstrators had achieved a great victory without firing a shot. They had forced by peaceful means an all–powerful government and the party into a full retreat. The old guard was gone. The new leadership was prepared to open the political system slowly to competing forces, and to listen much more closely to the demands of the people. Hans Modrow, the minister–president, and Hans Gysi, the party leader, had a political program with three major points:[5]

1. To preserve East Germany as an independent state, although some kind of closer relationship with West Germany seemed to be unavoidable;

2. To preserve the socialistic system by transforming the existing communist system (*Realsozialismus*) into a "democratic socialism" or "humane socialism"; and

3. To preserve a majority position for the former communist party in the upcoming free election.

This program met the aspirations of many of the new political groups. From those groups, the "New Forum" emerged as a kind of umbrella organization, one that was strongly influenced by clerics, teachers, and environmentalists.[6] The New Forum and most of the other political groups wanted East Germany to become a true socialist state in which the people and the environment were at the center of all state and private activity. These groups did not want to give up East Germany's independence and were convinced that their state would have enough of its own identity to survive as a neighbor of the capitalistic West Germany.

It was not surprising that these new political groups favored socialism and an independent East Germany. For years the East German government had permitted some freedom of expression to churches, left-leaning intellectuals, and environmentalists. These groups were therefore prepared when the demonstrations began and became the spokespersons of the first protest wave. Now, the state provided them with another platform and a larger audience.

The old democratic parties that still existed were virtually silent at this time. They had worked together with the communists in parliament and had argued that by doing so they had been able to water down many of the communist intentions. Now they tried to distance themselves from the communists. They did not want to embrace the positions of the New Forum, and a third position was not yet available.

However, it was not at all certain that the majority of the East Germans still wanted an independent socialist state, even one with some stronger links to West Germany. The opening of the Berlin Wall on the ninth of November and the subsequent breakdown of the border between East and West Germany formed a watershed event. More than one-third of all East Germans travelled into West Germany, received welcome money of DM 100 (about $65), and returned home with plastic bags of Western goods. These visitors did more than purchase consumer goods. They also had discussions, looked around, and learned more about politics in the East and the West than they had in years. Suddenly on November 22, at the by-then traditional Monday demonstrations in Leipzig, banners appeared which said, "We Germans are one people" and the demonstrators called for the unification of Germany.[7] At another rally, where Willy Brandt was guest of honor, a sign read, "Willy, no more socialism." The Wickert Institute, in a poll in mid-November, found to its great surprise that 67 percent of those interviewed favored unification over the continuation of the reform of their communist state. The suddenness of this change of direction in the demonstrators' demands cannot be overemphasized. The desire for unification must have been in the minds of many people for a long time, but it burst into the open only after people could see with their own eyes the differences between East and West Germany. The removal of the Berlin Wall had a great impact on the people's perceptions, for it led them to formulate much further reaching political goals.

Modrow suggested a "contractual community" (*Vertragsgemeinschaft*) between East and West Germany and hoped that he could get substantial financial support from West Germany for the "concession" of closer cooperation. Such a contractual community required creating a legal framework for the cooperation of two independent and equal states. Modrow hoped that this would satisfy his people and allow East Germany to continue to exist.

Modrow's program failed to gain the support of the majority of the East German people. He made serious mistakes in his effort to do both—gain the trust of the East German people and transform, not destroy, existing state organizations. When he suggested the creation of a new state security agency, modeled after West Germany's institutions, the East Germans realized how much Modrow, the former communist, was obligated to make compromises with former state officials. Modrow argued with hindsight that this was the moment when he lost the needed public support and when public opinion turned against him.[8] The demonstrations continued and the demands sharpened. The media revealed more and more details of the corruptness of the former communist regime and accused many officeholders and high–level bureaucrats of having had these privileges. The impression became pervasive that the old guard was still in control and working more for the rescue of their positions than for a genuine new beginning. Since the economic and political situation declined precipitously, the public distanced itself more and more from Modrow and his goal of the survival of East Germany as an independent state.

On January 30, 1990, Modrow went to Moscow and got Gorbachev's okay for the contractual community between East and West Germany. With this assurance, he went to Bonn and requested DM 15 billion ($9.7 billion) in support of his plan. But Kohl, realizing that Modrow had lost the trust and support of his people, outmaneuvered him in the international arena.

After the ninth of November when the Berlin Wall came down, Western governments could no longer be mere bystanders. Whether they wanted to or not, they became involved. The course and speed of events were breathtaking. Nobody had ever seen a regime vanish that had seemed so firmly in control only months before. Was the status quo really coming to an end and the border between East and West disappearing? By mid–November, the European governments realized that the status quo was actually breaking down. Most of them suggested that West Germany should financially support the democratization process in East Germany. Their goal was to postpone unification until it could occur as part of a larger European integration. They wanted West Germany to support East Germany financially so that the unification would not occur "prematurely," forced by economic distress in East Germany.

The position of François Mitterrand was representative of the opinions in the main European capitals. On December 6, in a meeting with Gorbachev in Kiev, Mitterrand argued that two sovereign German states were needed for the time being.[9] A week later, he explained to President Bush on the island of St. Martin that he intended to delay any German efforts toward unification. To do so, Mitterrand went to East Berlin on December 20, 1989, and publicly assured the new East German President of French support for the future existence of East Germany. The West German–French relations suffered from Mitterrand's outspoken opposition to any form of unification. Bonn needed one of the four victorious allies as a supporter of its unification efforts if it wanted to be successful.

Not only the world but also the West German politicians and the West German people were divided over this issue of unification.

The idea of a socialist East German state found support among West German intellectuals and left–leaning politicians. The Greens passed a resolution opposing reunification. Their opposition was joined by a sizable part of the SPD, in particular by Oskar Lafontaine, the party candidate for chancellor in the 1990 election. Their main arguments were that East Germany's socialistic/democratic way had values that should not be destroyed, that Germany should not aspire to regain its former political and economic strength that had brought so much grief to the world, and finally that the costs of unification would be too big a burden for the West Germans. Only Willy Brandt, the honorary chairman of the SPD, loudly and clearly said what many older SPD members must have felt: at the SPD Party Congress in

Berlin on Deccmber 18, he declared, "What belongs together is now growing together." And he warned other countries—and in particular, the four victorious allies—that:

> Nowhere is it written that the Germans have to remain stuck on a siding until the all–European train has reached the station.[10]

The conservative West German parties were principally committed to unification but did not believe that the chance for achieving it had yet arrived.

Even many West Germans who did not belong to the left were not so sure whether they wanted immediate unification or not. Many believed it would impose a tremendous financial burden on them and were uncertain whether it would be worth the price. But the personal encounters between East and West Germans had an effect on public opinion in West Germany. More and more people began supporting Kohl's efforts for early unification.[11]

On November 28, Chancellor Kohl made his move. Without first consulting either the Western partners or his opposition parties, he announced in one of his most important addresses in the Bundestag his "10–point program for unification." This program entailed a confederation for an interim period but the goal was clear: East Germany should disappear as an independent state and West Germany's system of democracy and capitalism should rule over all of Germany.[12]

On February 10, just before Modrow's visit to Bonn, Kohl and Gorbachev met in Moscow and talked privately for four hours. Kohl convinced his host that the East Germans should have the right to decide for themselves whether they wanted to live in one unified German state. Still in Moscow, Kohl proudly said in a news conference:

> Tonight, I have a single message for all Germans. Secretary Gorbachev and I agree that the German people have the right to decide for themselves whether they want to live together in one state. . . . This is great day for Germany and for me personally.[13]

After his visit to Moscow, Kohl knew that the East German state was finished. He was convinced that he would get unification on his terms and that any concession to the reformed communists would be counterproductive.[14] He sent Modrow home empty handed. The East German people understood that every penny would only have strengthened the chances of survival of the Modrow regime and would not have helped to bring about the desired unification. After Modrow's unsuccessful visit in Bonn, 300,000 East Germans gave Kohl the warmest reception of his political career. From then on, Kohl never wavered in the pursuit of unification.

Kohl's greatest political strength is to feel intuitively where public opinion is moving. Much earlier than others, he realized that on the ninth of November the reform movement had suddenly developed into a revolution.[15] The purpose of the reform movement had been to open and transform the communist system. The aim of the revolution was to destroy the communist system and the communist state. In past revolutions, the ruling class was physically liquidated and new forces took over the leadership. This time around, the ruling class was not liquidated but pushed aside. It was a revolution, nonetheless, because new forces became the political leaders of the country. The bloodless nature of the revolution had both its advantage and its disadvantage. The advantage was that the civil disruptions were minimal and no outside force—the Soviet army, for example—had an excuse to intervene. It is one of the miracles of the East German revolution that it occurred peacefully and that the people understood that disciplined and peaceful demonstrations in front of TV cameras were their strongest weapon. The disadvantage was that many communists were able to hide and to remain in important positions inside the administration. This hampered the transformation process and caused a lot of finger pointing after the democratic forces had taken over.

It must be said again that the watershed event was the opening of the Berlin Wall. Communist civilization did not survive the frontal clash with the much more successful democratic one. The East German people intuitively decided that their future would be much better as part of the democratic/capitalistic order. The communists and the original organizers of the reform movement lost control over the masses. New more visionary goals suddenly emerged center stage. The people of East Gemany became the driving force because the Modrow government and the world wanted to avoid chaos at the sensitive border between East and West and were willing to accommodate the people's demands as much as possible. Then Chancellor Kohl joined the East German people and made unification his personal goal. He soon took the initiative away from them and skillfully influenced the further proceedings. He masterfully used the favorable international environment and the revolutionary elan for the realization of an early unification.

C. The Election of March 18, 1990

The revolution succeeded. The communist ruling class was removed from office not by force but by an election. More and more of the revolutionary energies of the people were absorbed by the unfolding election campaign, and the Modrow government did not resist the democratization process. It was generally believed that Modrow and his supporters would give up their positions peacefully if the elections went against him and the PDS.

The communist party, now called the Party of Democratic Socialism (PDS), used its strong organizational base and the state–controlled propaganda apparatus for its election campaign. The PDS expected to gain enough votes to be a force that could not be overlooked in the next government–building process and had every reason to believe it would reach its goal. It was the only party in East Germany with a country–wide organization, a loyal party base (albeit smaller than a year earlier), and access to the state propaganda apparatus. With the support of the government bureaucracy, it could hamper the publicity efforts of competing parties. The PDS wanted elections to be held as soon as possible, knowing that such a schedule would give the other parties less time to prepare for an election. In November 1989, when the date for the elections was set, the competition was made up of dozens of small groups and parties that together were unlikely to gain the majority with its subsequent power in the new democratic state.

In 1989, when it suddenly became possible to engage in political activities outside the communist party, it was as if a dam had opened.[1] Political groups emerged everywhere, some intending to become national parties, others intending to remain as local discussion groups. As it turned out, twenty–four parties or associations participated in the March 18 election.[2] All of the smaller groups and parties were ill–prepared for a country–wide election campaign. Many of them had no office, no structure, and no knowledge of how to organize an election campaign. Many lacked such basic needs as typewriters and copy machines. Most of their representatives were known only at the local level, with programs too vague to be packaged into campaign messages.

The electoral law had not stipulated a 5 percent hurdle for entering parliament. Every representative who received a quarter of 1 percent of the votes was seated in parliament. This rule gave the small parties a chance for representation in the first democratically elected parliament and at least a small voice in the upcoming negotiations with West Germany about the unification. But these small parties could not expect to become a decisive force for shaping the future. With some resignation, their leaders realized that the fruits of the revolution had been taken away from them. Even if they combined forces, they stood no chance of winning a meaningful portion of the votes. A majority of East Germans shared their opposition to the communist regime but not their dream of a truly democratic-socialistic society. Only their best known representatives had the chance to win a seat in parliament and thus continue to be heard in the future.

The communists had judged correctly. The small revolutionary parties were no match for the PDS, which would have won an important share of parliament seats if the traditional parties had not made a strong comeback.

In 1945 and 1946, the communists had destroyed the independence of the old and well–known democratic parties; but, with the exception of the SPD, they did not eliminate them from the political process. They allowed the Christian–Democratic Party (CDU), the Liberal Party (LDP), the National–Democratic Party (NDP), and the Democratic Peasant Party to continue a controlled existence because they were useful as a democratic facade. The continued existence of conservative parties gave some credence to the official name of the state, the "German Democratic Republic." The bourgeois parties never voted against government proposals in parliament; thus, the question was raised whether they represented their constituencies at all. They argued that they were effective because they forced the communists to make concessions *before* the votes were taken in parliament and that their survival was essential for a new beginning after the communist era. The East German people never trusted those arguments. They called the communist and the conservative parties the "Bloc–parties," a name meant to imply that the East Germans always believed that these parties cooperated for their mutual benefit, not for the best of the people. How these parties should organize their new beginning under democratic rules was a very difficult question.

In 1945, the SPD was forbidden because it was the direct competitor of the communists for the representation of the working class.[3] As a consequence of this demise, the SPD was no part of the ruling elite and so its comeback in 1989 was relatively easy. On October 7, 1989, forty people founded the East German SPD anew, claiming to be the successor organization to the party forbidden in 1945. The new founders were not tainted by prior cooperation with the communist regime, so the new SPD easily won credibility among the East German people. The party flourished, and by January 1990 it already had a membership of 70,000.

When it became clear in January of 1990 that Germans would be united, the West German parties also wanted to be part of the democratic beginning in East Germany. They wanted to participate in the March 18 election in East Germany because they knew that the winners of that election would negotiate the unification with West Germany. The West German SPD simply embraced its East German sister organization. With their great size and democratic experience, the West Germans easily took control. Suddenly, typewriters and copy machines were available. Almost overnight, the SPD became a serious competitor against the PDS.[4] Opinion polls taken by the Allensbach Institute in January/February predicted an impressive victory for the SPD. At that time, 50 percent of the population planned to vote for the SPD.[5]

But the SPD had a major problem that caused it eventually to lose its lead. It was disunited about the only issue that counted in this election. The man designated to be the SPD candidate for chancellor in the West German election planned for 1990, Oskar Lafontaine, campaigned for a "go–slow" approach to unification.[6] Willy Brandt, the honorary chairman of the SPD, campaigned for the unification. And so did Ibrahim Boehme, the East German SPD party leader. Inside the SPD, the rift was so deep that Lafontaine was asked to limit his appearances in East Germany.

The bourgeois parties had great difficulties embracing their East German counterparts. Both the F.D.P. and the CDU requested that the East German parties had first to elect a new slate of representatives before a partnership with campaign support and the goal of party unification was feasible. The Western bourgeois parties did not want to be seen cooperating with functionaries who supported the communist regime. Only through the pressure from the West did the East German parties eventually get rid of their old leadership and elect fresh faces. Thus the partnership was consumated relatively late. A slow and belated start of their election campaign was the result.[7]

The F.D.P., confronted with three liberal parties in East Germany, persuaded them to enter into the "Federation of Free Democrats" and to announce that a formal merger would soon be consumated.[8] But the F.D.P. made the tactical error of putting its West German credo and slogans at center stage. They campaigned with the slogans of individualism and the free-market system, without realizing that these were alien concepts for most East Germans. The East Germans were not ready to accept individualism with all its opportunities and risks. Thus, the F.D.P. came away disappointed from this election although their locomotive was Hans-Dietrich Genscher, the West German foreign minister, one of the architects of unification and a native of their own country.

The Christian Democratic Party (CDU) had to wait longer than the F.D.P. before the leadership question of the East-CDU was resolved. A considerable amount of time passed before the old CDU guard abdicated and Lothar de Maiziere, a lawyer and violist, became the head of the East-CDU. Only then was the West-CDU prepared to cooperate. But barely a day after this had happened, the West-CDU took over the election campaign—just as the other West German parties had done before. East Germany became a battleground for the West German parties, and the East Germans were stunned by the aggressiveness and divisiveness of a democratic election campaign.

Chancellor Kohl was the great drawing card of the CDU. He visited East Germany five times, receiving the most enthusiastic welcomes of his political career. The East Germans intuitively understood that Kohl and his concept worked in their favor and that the hesitations of other politicians were detrimental to their cause.[9]

Professor Noelle-Neumann closely watched the change of public opinion. Surprised by the speed and degree of change, she wrote:

> Weeks were like years. Not that they passed so slowly; quite the contrary. In the last four weeks before the election, public opinion changed more profoundly and more quickly than ever observed by opinion research before.[10]

The SPD, which would have been the clear winner at the

beginning of January, lost its leading position. The CDU, which had been so far behind that nobody gave it a chance of becoming the strongest party, gained from week to week. The PDS seemed able to hold on to a hard core of supporters during these turbulent times:

Percent of the Population Favoring One Party[11]

	Feb. 18	March 8	March 15	Election
PDS (Communists)	18	18	18	16.3
SPD(Social–Democrats)	48	37	27	21.8
CDU (Christian–Democrats)	21	34	45	48.2

The democratic process had worked. The East Germans were presented with clear choices between very different economic and political programs. The information, albeit presented in shrill campaign messages, reached the audience. Twelve million two hundred thousand East Germans had the right to vote. Four hundred parliamentary seats were at stake. Of the eligible voters, 99.3 percent voluntarily went to the polls and voted for their representatives who in turn had to elect the government. The election outcome, although it had been predicted by opinion research, was still a great surprise to the people and even to the politicians:

The Election in East Germany on March 18, 1990[12]

	% of Votes	Seats in Parliament
CDU	40.9	164
DSU	6.3	25
DA	.9	4
Federation of Free Democrats	5.3	21
SPD	21.8	87
Buednis 90 (New Forum, etc.)	2.9	12
PDS (Former Communists)	16.3	65
Small Groups or Parties	5.6	22
	100.0	400

These election results were accepted in East Germany and abroad because people believed the elections were fair and held without government interference. They were taken as a mandate to continue work toward early unification and to wipe out the communist past in East Germany.

The East German CDU and its leader, Lothar de Maiziere, had won the public mandate to form the first government.[13] De Maiziere decided not to follow the West German example and to put a conservative–liberal coalition in place. He opted for a grand coalition because he wanted all major democratic forces to work together for the great goal of unification.[14] He hoped thereby to minimize public resistance to unpopular decisions that the new government would certainly have to make in the near future. He also wanted to look as strong as possible vis-à-vis his West German negotiation partners. However, the SPD was so shocked with its dismal election outcome that it took several weeks before the party was ready to take over government responsibility. The SPD realized that the alternative, staying out of the government, was even less attractive, for it would have shared the opposition role with the PDS. In opposition, the SPD might have become the weaker force, because the SPD supported the unification in principle and the PDS did not. A government without the SPD would still have commanded an impressive majority in parliament and would in all likelihood have negotiated successfully with West Germany (though the acceptance of these negotiation results would have been accompanied by longer and perhaps more divisive debates in the East German parliament). In the end, those laws would have passed because even if the SPD and tje PDS would have voted together, they still did not command enough votes to prevent their acceptance in parliament.

At the beginning of May, East Germany's first democratically elected government was in place and the negotiations for the unification could begin.[15] The East German people had driven the communists from power and had installed a government to negotiate the unification. In a sense, their part of the revolution was finished. Now the people expected that their government and the trusted Chancellor of West Germany would take over and fulfill the obligation of unification. Nonetheless, the truce between the government and the people was somewhat uneasy. Both sides knew that to disappoint the people's expectations could immediately cause the resumption of the flight to West Germany that would further destabilize East Germany.

Thus, the East and West German governments were under pressure to produce a positive outcome in a reasonable period of time.

III. THE UNIFICATION OF GERMANY

A. The Problems Surrounding the Unification

Germany's unification raised both internal and international questions. The important internal question was how to put together two states that over forty years had developed very different political, economic, and social systems and whose living standards were far apart from each other.

West German politicians advanced two models for the unification. Oskar Lafontaine, the chancellor candidate of the SPD, wanted the two German states to remain in existence for an indefinite period of time, until they became slowly linked together by common political institutions that would gain weight with the passing of time.[1] He argued that although both states were democratically ruled, they had very different economic and social systems that should be brought together slowly. He expected that both states should give up some of their characteristic features and through adaptation create a new system, one somewhere in the middle between capitalism and socialism. The so-called "third way" should finally emerge. Basically, Lafontaine wanted to use East Germany as a lever to change West Germany into a society where solidarity would gain the upper hand over competition.

In other words, the old socialistic dream remained strong. The socialist had never stopped distrusting the market forces and the discipline of a competitive system. Solidarity among people and a state which cared for all eventualities of life were the still cherished socialistic goals.

Lafontaine also argued that West Germany should support East Germany financially until the gap between their living standards narrowed. Since time would be required to merge the economic and social systems and to narrow the gap in living standards, unification would have been postponed indefinitely. Lafontaine wanted the unification to coincide with the creation of a greater Europe, one that encompassed the European community and the East European states. He believed that in such a larger entity a unified Germany would be less likely to have the leading position that its size and economic power would otherwise command. Lafontaine opposed nationalistic sentiments in Germany, arguing that the time for the emergence of an European identity and feeling had arrived. Because of its burdened past, Germany, he felt, should be the first nation to give up narrow, nationalistic attitudes.[2]

Lafontaine was convinced that in the March election the East Germans, coming from a communist system, would vote for a socialistic rather than a bourgeois government. He also hoped to beat Chancellor Kohl in the December 1990 West German election. With social democratic leaders in place in both states, Lafontaine felt sure he could transform the capitalistic system in the West and the communist system in the East into a mutually compatible system, closely resembling the Swedish socialist model.

Lafontaine's model was eagerly embraced by other leftist forces and by a large number of left–leaning intellectuals. The Greens passed a resolution opposing the outright unification of Germany.

But in the SPD itself, Lafontaine's vision was not universally accepted. Willy Brandt, for example, argued that the unification should not be artificially delayed and believed that the German people were entitled to a reasonable degree of nationalistic feeling—like any other European nation. He and many other social–democrats were torn between party discipline on the one hand and, on the other, their recognition that the bourgeois model for unification was much closer to their personal convictions than the model presented and defended by their own chancellor candidate.

The bourgeois model for the unification of Germany was based on the conviction that the West German economic and social system had proven its superior merits, while the East German system was demonstrably corrupt and ineffective.[3] Therefore, the disappearance of the East German state would not be a loss to the East German people and the world. The East Germans would become part of West Germany, and the West German system of government would be introduced in its place with as little adjustment and as few transitional regulations as possible. The bourgeois goal was unification on West Germany's terms as soon as possible. The pressure to more rapidly unite was caused by the continuing economic deterioration in East

Germany. The bourgeois parties also rejected support payments to the reform communists, for those payments would only fortify communist power and postpone the necessary transformation to political and economic freedom.

These two models competed for acceptance not only in both Germanies but also in the world at large. Within Germany, they became part of the election campaign that divided the country into two unequal camps. The world at large, the European neighbors of Germany in the East and West in particular, would have preferred Lafontaine's approach. But in the Spring of 1990, these countries realized that Lafontaine's fortunes were slipping while Kohl's were on the rise. Only the U. S. supported Kohl's position from the outset.

The unification of Germany posed three clusters of international problems. The first cluster entailed problems of future superpower relations. The second cluster entailed the questions arising from the fact that East and West Germany were the border states of the Warsaw Pact and of NATO respectively.[4] The third cluster of questions dealt with the problem of how to fit a larger and more powerful Germany into the existing European institutions.

At the beginning of June, the foreign ministers of East and West Germany met in Bonn with the foreign ministers of the victorious allies of World War II—U. S., Britain, France, and the Soviet Union. At this first "two–plus–four meeting," Shevardnadze, then foreign minister of the Soviet Union, proposed separating the internal and the international questions from each other so that Germany could unite without the delays that waiting for the solution of the international questions might cause.[5] West Germany's foreign minister, Hans–Dietrich Genscher, liked this proposal, but Helmut Kohl did not accept it.[6] Supported by U. S. Secretary of State James Baker, Kohl argued that the unification and the restoration of the full sovereignty of Germany had to occur together. On this issue, the East German government also backed Kohl's position. For East Germany, the lack of sovereignty remained a problem because Soviet occupation continued and people feared that the move to freedom could be aborted any time.

The internal and the international questions were not untied. As a result, a number of very different issues at very different levels needed to be addressed.[7] The German unification remained imbedded in the larger issues mentioned above, and many believed that unification would emerge as the final achievement of undoing this Gordian knot.

The superpowers and all other involved parties foresaw a lengthy and difficult negotiation process. Kohl, for example, said that he did not expect the unification to occur before 1991. But the world leaders lost control over the speed of the process. The people of East Germany once again determined the timetable. East German economic conditions deteriorated very fast in the summer of 1990, and world leaders realized that East Germany would not survive as a viable entity for any length of time. The Soviet Union, in particular, suddenly had to confront the question of whether to allow the border region of its hemisphere to sink into chaos or to speed up the negotiations with the West. The West simultaneously faced growing German pressure to allow unification to take place. Kohl argued that otherwise a unification of another sort would occur: millions of East Germans would migrate into West Germany and cause enormous problems on both sides of the border. In essence, the people of East Germany enforced the unification according to the bourgeois model in 1990. In this sense, the revolution continued until Germany was finally united.

B. The Settlement of the International Questions Surrounding the Unification

World War II and the division of the world into communist and democratic zones of influence created the German question. Germans, their politicians included, believed that the division of Germany into a Western and an Eastern half could be overcome by peaceful means only if and when the global political situation would change. West and East Germany needed, in German eyes, to lose their frontier-state characteristic before any kind of unification could become feasible. And even then, they believed, the unification would pose a severe problem because the Soviet Union would not give up such an important economic asset without compensation. That the West would give up West Germany was never considered.

To the great surprise of the world, Gorbachev's reform movement loosened Soviet control over Eastern Europe and provided a chance for the division of the world, and particularly of Europe, to be brought to a peaceful end.[1] Since the Reykjavik Summit in October of 1986, Gorbachev had been pleading for an overhaul of the global political situation. It took the U. S. administration until the Malta Summit in December of 1989 to accept that the changes in the communist hemisphere were genuine and that the Western world should react positively.[2] There were several specific issues for discussion between Bush and Gorbachev: the role of the superpowers, the defense pacts in the East and West, the future of Europe, and the role of international financial institutions. Both leaders agreed in these discussions that one of the final arrangements would be a settlement of the German question. In essence, Bush and Gorbachev hinted in Malta that the division of the world into two hostile or competing camps had a real chance of ending, to make room for the emergence of a new order.

Over the years since 1945, leaders in the East and the West had shown a strong desire to maintain the status quo in Europe and elsewhere. Had not the division in Europe along the iron curtain brought about stability and peace for forty–five years? People in the West had

grown accustomed to the status quo. Their living standard had risen
continually, and they enjoyed political stability and freedom. For the
people under communist rule, the situation was quite different. They
exploited the opening provided by *glasnost* and *perestroika*, toppled
their communist regimes, and tried to install new governments they
could trust. The East Germans went a big step further, demanding
not merely a new government but the disappearance of their state and
unification with West Germany. This made the German case unique
and completely different from the revolutions in Poland, Czechoslovakia, and Hungary.

The demand for unification created great emotional problems—
particularly for the other European countries. An incident in July
illuminated the severity of the problem.[3] Margaret Thatcher had sum-
moned some of the best known Western historians for a private conference about Germany. These experts urged Mrs. Thatcher to give up
her resistance to Germany's unification and to accept the fact that today's Germany was vastly different from the one in the past. Despite
this advice, Nicholas Ridley, Thatcher's trusted trade and industry
secretary, lashed out and bluntly expressed his opinion. Interviewed
in the London–based *Spectator*, he argued that, "This is all a German
racket designed to take over the whole of Europe." He compared Kohl
with Hitler and called the French "the German poodles" for changing
their minds and now supporting the German unification. Thatcher
had to settle this embarrassment by dismissing Ridley, but German
leaders were well aware that Ridley's sentiments were widely shared
in European capitals.

Resistance to the unification of Germany was well entrenched.
The current size of West Germany's population and its economic
power were similar to those of the other large European countries.
Adding some 16 million East Germans would create the largest and
economically strongest country of Europe. Rome, Paris, and London
were concerned that ambitious German politicians could translate
economic strength into the political domination of Europe. In East
European capitals, particularly in Warsaw, the fear was great that
a united Germany might become so attractive to German minorities
that they would want to discuss anew the Eastern border of Germany. Large parts of Silesia, for example, had been German territory
for centuries, although most of the Germans were driven away after
World War II. The economic data actually showed that a united Germany would have by far the largest economy in Europe and would be

the fourth largest in the world.

Germany in Comparison[4]
(1988 Figures)

	Population (millions)	Gross Domestic Product ($ billions)
USSR	280	2,535
U. S.	226	4,864
Japan	121	1,758
United Germany	78	1,077
Britain	57	755
France	57	754
Italy	56	762

Kohl understood very well that he had to present "confidence-building approaches" to overcome the resistance to the German unification by the other European countries. He generally reacted to these concerns by pointing out that Europe had a way to harness the greater German economic weight. The European Community needed only to speed up the process of its own economic and political integration. To demonstrate his good intentions, Kohl, supported by Mitterrand, suggested a strengthening of political cooperation within the European community.[5] Kohl also reiterated that decisions in Europe should be based on "one country, one vote," meaning that every member nation, whether large or small, should have the same weight.

Kohn and Hans–Dietrich Genscher, West Germany's foreign minister since 1974, were experienced enough not to overestimate Germany's political weight. They realized that alone, Germany's efforts would not suffice to overcome the open and hidden resistance in Europe and in the Soviet Union. They knew that they needed the support of the U. S., especially in their dealings with the Soviet Union. Germany chose and found in the U. S. its main support at the bargaining table with the other victorious allies.[6] From the very beginning, Genscher established a close working relationship with Secretary Baker and convinced him that it was in the best interests of the U. S. to support German unification.

It was not easy to put the unification of Germany on the international agenda. The breakthrough occurred in Ottawa on February 15, 1990, where twenty–three foreign ministers from NATO and the

Warsaw Pact nations gathered for their first joint meeting. Secretary Baker negotiated on behalf of the Germans. On February 16, the *New York Times* reported that:

> Britain, France, and the Soviet Union preferred that the four Allied powers discuss the future of Germany among themselves—and not, at first, with the Germans—but Washington talked them into bringing the Germans in from the start. Once the Germans were brought into the process, Bonn insisted on excluding the other nations of the 16-member North Atlantic Treaty Organization from these discussions.[7]

Genscher even got assurance that the "formula" would be "two–plus–four" and not "four–plus–two" as the British foreign minister had requested. The two–plus–four formula was supposed to indicate that the two Germanies would first determine the nature of their unification and only then deal with the Allied powers who still had overseeing rights and responsibilities in Germany.

How interrelated and complex the global, European, and German questions really were can best be seen in the timetable for top–level political meetings in the summer of 1990:

May 31–June 1	Summit Meeting between Bush and Gorbachev in Washington
June 7–June 8	Two–Plus–Four Meeting in Bonn
June 22	Two–plus–Four Meeting in East Berlin
June 25	EC–Summit Meeting in Dublin
July 5	NATO Meeting in London
July 9–July 11	Economic Summit Meeting in Houston
July 15–July 16	Meeting between Gorbachev and Kohl in Moscow and Stavropol
July 17	Two–Plus–Four Meeting in Paris
September 12	Two–Plus–Four Meeting in Moscow
October 1	CSCE Meeting in Washington

Although the NATO meeting in Ottawa brought the issue of German unification to the bargaining table, German unification could occur only if other international issues were first resolved.[9] The main players in these complex negotiations had basically the following interests:

1. Germany's interests were twofold. It wanted to:

(a) Achieve unification and full sovereignty.

(b) Remain firmly anchored in the Western family of nations.

2. The U. S. had the following interests:

(a) To continue to be an important power in Europe.

(b) NATO to survive and to keep U. S. troops on European soil in order to retain its image as the protector of a free Europe.

(c) To have a position in Europe superior to that of the USSR.

3. The Soviet Union had the following interests:

(a) It had a genuine security interest. The Soviet Union was in the process of losing the buffer zone beween its national border and the West. It wanted assurances that the West would respect its border as immutable for the indefinite future.

(b) It wanted to establish itself as an important European power.

(c) It wanted both superpowers to have an equal standing in Europe. For that, the Soviet Union suggested that both defense pacts, the Warsaw Pact and NATO, be dismantled and replaced by a newly created security umbrella under the Helsinki accord (CSCE).

4. Poland asked to be included in the negotiations because of its border with Germany.

5. The other European countries also wanted to participate in these negotiations about Germany's future.

Serious negotiations started at the superpower summit in Washington at the end of May 1990, the beginning of two months of intensive negotiations at all levels. During this period, the pressure for success intensified because the economic and political situation in East Germany deteriorated so rapidly. When these meetings began, the involved politicians believed that unification could wait until 1991. In July, they knew that the unification had to occur in 1990 if chaos were to be avoided.[10] During this period, the negotiators worked themselves almost to the point of exhaustion. *The Wall Street Journal* reported on July 18 that since May, Shevardnadze and Genscher had met ten times for a total of fifty hours at eight different locations to hammer out an amicable agreement.

At the end of May at the summit meeting in Washington, President Bush outlined the American position.[11] The U. S. insisted that a unified Germany had to be a member of the Western family of nations.

This meant that Germany had to remain in the European Community and in NATO. The U. S. supported by all Western nations, was unwilling to dismantle NATO simultaneously with the disintegrating Warsaw Pact.[12] But the U. S. was prepared to bend over backwards and to assure the Soviet Union that NATO's character was a defensive one.[13] The U. S. was even willing to adjust the wording of NATO's mission accordingly. But Gorbachev insisted that NATO and the Warsaw Pact were both creations of the Cold War and should be dismantled simultaneously. New security arrangements for Europe should be created with both superpowers represented equally. But Gorbachev could not prevail in Washington. His negotiating position was relatively weak. The Warsaw Pact was already in a state of dissolution, while NATO was still on a firm footing. And time was working against him as the crisis in East Germany deepened almost daily.

When Gorbachev failed to eliminate NATO, he asserted that a united Germany could not continue to be a member of this organization. This position found no approval in East and West European capitals, for an independent German military establishment was regarded as less desirable than a NATO that kept German military might under control. Thus, it was only a question of time before Gorbachev had to give in to the U. S. and had to change his position yet again. This time, he requested the permanent reduction of German military might, and he prevailed.

Throughout these negotiations, the U. S. and its allies had a much better negotiating position than the Soviet Union. The relationship between the U. S. and Europe was based not only on military ties but first and foremost on a common heritage of freedom and democracy. This philosophical commonality endured when the need for military ties declined in importance. Europe did not forget that the U. S. had come as a liberator. On the other hand, the Soviet Union remained burdened with the image of having been an oppressor. Even Gorbachev's Western style could not gloss over this fundamental difference. Last, but not least, the Eastern half was on the verge of disintegration. The Soviet Union was under pressure to resolve an escalating problem at its Western border, while the West could afford to wait until Moscow offered the right conditions for a settlement.

The U. S. and its Western allies, Germany included, achieved their original goals. The Soviet Union did not, but managed to gain a substantial number of concessions. On July 17, 1990, at the two-plus-four meeting in Paris, the Soviet Union agreed that a united Germany could remain in the Western fold, that NATO could remain as the security umbrella of the West, and that Germany could stay in NATO.[14] In return, the door was opened for a reformed Soviet Union to became integrated into Europe and into the family of democratically oriented nations. The mission of NATO was newly formulated, stressing even more its defensive character. Germany's military power was permanently reduced. Large sums of economic aid were promised to the Soviet Union, from Germany in particular. A foundation was laid for the disappearance of the division of Europe into East and West. The iron curtain and the Berlin Wall became symbols of a past that should never be repeated.

The breakthrough in the negotiations between East and West came in a meeting between Gorbachev and Kohl in Moscow and Stavropol on July 15 and 16. In the private atmosphere of the Caucasus Mountains, Kohl was able to convince Gorbachev of the need to acquiesce to the Western position. In exchange, Kohl offered generous economic support, a limitation of Germany's military might, and the prospect that close economic cooperation between Germany and the Soviet Union might emerge.[16] In essence, the Soviet Union gave up a bankrupt East Germany in exchange for the goodwill of the unified Germany.

West German obligations and contributions to this settlement were very specific. Germany obligated itself to maintaining only a small army, one that would allow the nation to defend itself but too weak to attack neighboring countries. The agreed limit of 370,000 men in the prospective German army makes it smaller than the Polish army of 500,000. No NATO troops will be stationed in the territory that was formerly East Germany. Soviet troops will be allowed to remain in East Germany until 1994. Germany has also agreed to spend up to DM 12 billion ($7.75 billion) to construct housing and other non-military facilities in the Soviet Union for the returning troops.[17]

Germany and the Soviet Union also initialed a twenty-year "Treaty on Good Neighborliness, Partnership, and Cooperation." According to this agreement, Germany will provide generous financial and technical help for the reconstruction of the Soviet economy. Kohl was also one of the outspoken supporters of a $15 billion "Marshall Plan" for the Soviet Union at the EC-Summit meeting in Dublin and at the

NATO meeting in London.

A very concerned party to these negotiations were the Poles. Their deepest concern was their border with Germany. Poland's worries were laid to rest at the Paris two–plus–four meeting in July 1990.[18] It received assurances of the inviolability of its Western border, as well as some economic concessions. This removed the last obstacle to a settlement of the international questions surrounding the unification. Thus, on September 12, 1990, at the last scheduled two–plus–four meeting in Moscow, the six foreign ministers in the presence of Mr. Gorbachev signed the "Treaty on the Final Settlement with Respect to Germany."

The U. S. had reached its goals, since the Warsaw Pact was dissolved and NATO remained intact. Germany had received international consent to unite in full sovereignty and solidly integrated into the West. The other Western European countries were assured by treaty that Germany would remain anchored in multinational institutions, thus diluting some of its potential economic power and political clout. Poland received international guarantees regarding its border. The world seemed to have succeeded in moving in an orderly, well–negotiated fashion from the period of superpower confrontation into a period in which the dividing line between East and West could disappear and a new global system for the post superpower era could emerge.

The "Treaty on the Final Settlement With Respect to Germany" was presented to the Conference on Security and Cooperation in Europe (CSCE) in New York on October 1, 1990, and endorsed. With this, an important chapter of the postwar history came to an end.

The treaty could not be ratified by the governments involved in time for the actual unification of Germany on October 3; but, in a well–received gesture, the four victorious Allies signed a document stating that they would no longer exercise their occupation rights. This cleared the way for Germany to unite in full sovereignty. Thereafter, the Allied troops that remained in Berlin were there by a special invitation of the German government.

The period from September of 1989 to October of 1990 presented a unique opportunity for the unification of Germany. At that time, no one knew whether this opportunity would remain open for a longer period of time; so it was important that the political leaders moved quickly to take advantage of this somewhat unexpected opening. Kohl and Genscher must be credited for their sensitivity in realizing that the time had come to press for the realization of a goal envisioned by German politicians since 1949. The efforts of Kohl and Genscher were strongly supported by the East German people who made it clear to the world that they regarded unacceptable anything less than unification and that they were prepared to leave their country at the first sign that unification would be postponed. The victorious Allies, the Soviets in particular, were greatly influenced by this threat. Thus, the East Germans themselves made a large contribution to the final outcome and the rapid realization of the unification.

C. The Economic, Social, and Monetary Union

The East German people wanted, and Chancellor Kohl had promised, an early unification. Kohl expected this process, mostly involving the resolution of the surrounding international problems, to take about a year; thus, the unification was presumed to occur in 1991. But the rapid decay in East Germany considerably shortened the time available for negotiations. The situation became so desperate that Kohl was forced to make a symbolic statement that was strong enough to stabilize the circumstances in East Germany.

By January 1990, it had already been decided that the bourgeois, not the social–democatic, model of unification would be followed; but there were different ways to achieve that general goal. The East German people strongly favored a process that would give them early access to the West German consumer market and leave as much purchasing power in their hands as possible. In essence, they wanted the Deutsche Mark to became legal tender and replace their own currency as soon as possible. Their public demands greatly influenced Kohl's decision. In order to avoid a breakdown of East Germany, the unification was divided into an economic and a political part, a division which made it possible to appease the East German public by economic unification without forcing the negotiating allies to come up with a solution to the surrounding international problems at the same time.[1]

Decoupling the economic and political unification entailed great risks for Germany and for Kohl's political career. Economic unification was expected to stabilize the econonic conditions in East Germany. Since East German economic instability was one of the reasons the Allied forces, and the Soviet Union in particular, were prepared to end the unnatural division of Germany, economic stability could have the unwelcome effect for Kohl of removing that force for change. Internally, Kohl provided much money and invested his prestige and political future by introducing the DM even though he did not, and could not, have political control over the whole process. Kohl took these risks both externally and internally.

His decision to start the process of unification by introducing the Deutsche Mark in East Germany was not without opposition. Even his own advisors were split about the political expediency of this move. For example, Karl-Otto Poehl, president of the Deutsche Bundesbank (Federal Reserve Board), advised a slow process of unification with the monetary exchange of East Mark into West Mark coming only at the end. Poehl also recommended an exchange rate of three East Marks for one West Mark as prudent, since statistics suggested that the productivity of an East German worker was only about one-third of that of his West German counterpart.[2] Poehl wanted East Germany to have a competitive advantage over the highly industrialized West Germany after the unification. He believed that this edge was needed for the emergence of a private investment boom that, in turn, was thought to be the major condition for rapid economic development of this "underdeveloped" region.[3]

Poehl's opinion was shared by many other economic experts, most of whom believed that first a democratic socio-economic system would have to be installed before the East German currency should be replaced by the West German one.[4] This replacement should be accompanied by a sharp reduction in the nominal value of private savings. The East Germans had amassed a relatively high amount of private savings because so little was available in their stores, and West German experts feared that this purchasing-power overhang, if generously exchanged, would suddenly hit their markets, creating an inflationary, albeit temporary, boom. Therefore, they argued, East German savings needed to be reduced. This position was not as unfair as it sounds. West German consumer goods (such as autos, refrigerators, and TVs) were readily available and much cheaper than they had been in communist East Germany. Thus, even the savings which would remain in private hands after devaluation would still purchase a relatively large amount of amenities.

In contrast with such critics, Chancellor Kohl realized that the deterioration of East Germany was so rapid that an orderly transition was no longer possible. He felt that the strongest possible signal was needed to stabilize the situation and to instill new confidence. Whether economically correct or not, Kohl decided that the strongest signal of all would be the immediate introduction of the DM in East Germany. Before the March election, Kohl announced that the process of unification would start with the introduction of the Deutsche

Mark (DM) as legal tender in East Germany on July 2.[5] As he had expected, that was the sign the East Germans had waited for. The DM, like the Mercedes star, was and is the symbol of West Germany's success.

In another sense, it was also a clever move to start the unification with a monetary reform. It revived memories, for in 1949, the West German economic miracle also started with monetary reform and the introduction of the DM. Everyone who had lived at that time remembered that before the reform, nothing was available in the stores. On the very day when DM became the legal tender, stores suddenly had consumer goods on their shelves. Most Germans in the East and West expected such a miracle to happen again.

Kohl had made the correct decision. The announcement that the DM would be introduced in a very short period of time averted a crisis. The flow of East Germans into West Germany came to a halt, and West Germany was even able to cut its subsidies for newcomers without causing disappointment among East Germans.[6] A cooling–off period started during which serious negotiations about the details of the unification were undertaken.

The negotiations for the economic, social, and monetary unification went very well. The March election brought a CDU–led coalition government into power in East Berlin. CDU politicians on both sides of the table helped to overcome the difficulties. Both negotiation partners wanted success and realized that they had to arrive at an amicable compromise in a relatively short period of time, before new public anxieties might arise. On May 18, only a month after the election, the treaty was signed in Bonn.[7] As Kohl foretold, the date for the economic unification and the introduction of the DM was to be Monday, July 2, 1990.

The underlying idea of the treaty was for East Germany to change its economic and social system from a planned to a free system at once. West Germany's economic and social laws and regulations would be introduced immediately with as few changes as possible. The transition would be facilitated by the immediate introduction of the much more generous West German social security and welfare system. Large amounts of money would be made available to cover initial government expenditures and for immediate investments into the crumbling infrastructure. These government–initiated investments were supposed to bridge the time until private investments into businesses and properties would become the motor for growth. The monetary reform would be generous, leaving substantial purchasing power in the hands of East Germans. This would assure not only positive acceptance by the population but also an immediate economic push by purchases of consumer goods. The officials were convinced that, as in 1949, the retail trade would have consumer goods readily available on July 2. In essence, officials believed they had set the stage for an immediate economic recovery in East Germany.

To finance this start into a democratic future, the West German federal and state governments set up the "Unity Fund" of DM 115 billion ($74.2 billion).[8] The negotiations team had calculated that the East German deficits—DM 30 billion ($19.3 billion) in 1990 and DM 50 billion ($32 billion) in 1991—should be financed by the unity fund. Additional funds were earmarked for early investments.

Much public speculation preceded the decision about the exchange rate of East Mark into Deutsche Mark. In November 1989, the East Mark had fallen as low as 20 : 1 on the black market, but later stabilized at 3 : 1, reflecting the differential in productivity. The overwhelming majority of East Germans were not impressed by the productivity argument and argued that an exchange of 3 : 1 would punish them, the weaker part of the Germans who had already experienced severe disadvantages for forty–five years. A different way should be found to make them competitive with their Western brothers. They strongly demanded an exchange of 1 : 1 or at least of 2 : 1. Chancellor Kohl, seeing that economic prudence and political reality were not congruent, decided in favor of political expediency.[9] Basically he promised that a major portion of the private savings, the first DM 6,000 ($3,870) for every person, would be exchanged at the favorable rate of 1 : 1. Additional savings and other than private savings would be exchanged at a rate of 2 : 1. Since most East Germans, after distributing their savings among all family members, did not have more than the initial DM 6,000, the exchange of almost all private savings occurred at the rate of 1 : 1.

This rate left a substantial amount of purchasing power in private hands. In total, savings were reduced from 182.1 billion East Marks to 123.3 billion Deutsche Marks.[10] That is, the population and businesses nominally lost 32.3 percent; but in reality, they gained in purchasing power, compared with the purchasing power of their former currency. All debts were cut in half. In total, 447 billion East Marks were converted into 246 billion Deutsche Marks. This meant on the average, each 1.8 East Mark became 1 DM.

The Deutsche Bundesbank, the supervisory authority for German banks and the protector of monetary stability, was the organizer of the monetary exchange.[11] This task was executed with the expected diligence. East Germans needed a bank account for the monetary exchange; no currency was accepted. The authorities knew that families had divided their savings so that each family member got the favorable 1 : 1 exchange rate. The waiting lines in front of the banks were reasonable, even festive, on the second of July. For the most part, people did not go on a buying binge, although most Western goods were suddenly available. Beneath the festive atmosphere lay a certain amount of anxiety about what the future might hold. Many people realized that they had lived poor but protected lives and understood that from then on, their own initiative would decide their well–being and their position in the society. On July 2, the East Germans knew that they had embarked on the difficult road to a new way of life, that it would take great efforts to reach the comfortable lifestyle of West Germany.

In summary, in February, Chancellor Kohl took the anxieties of the East Germans seriously and acceded to their request that something important and irreversible must be done immediately. He separated the unification into an economic and a political part. By doing so, he hoped to stop the rapid economic deterioration in East Germany and to give himself and the world the chance to orderly negotiate the global implications of the unification. With hindsight, it is clear that Kohl had the best political sensitivity. By listening to the people in East Germany and not to experts, he succeeded and brought about an orderly unification.

D. The Economic Recovery That Did Not Materialize

The monetary reform elicited two opposing predictions. On the one side, the opposition parties, especially Oskar Lafontaine, argued that an economic breakdown would follow and that the money provided by West Germany was insufficient to bridge the economic abyss between the past and the future. On the other side, the ruling coalition and its supporters voiced the optimistic prediction that a recovery would instantly unfold, as it had in 1949 when the DM was introduced in West Germany.[1]

As it turned out, however, the past looked brighter in retrospect than it really was. Also the situation of 1949 and 1990 could not be compared. In 1949, everyone in West Germany was poor and eager to improve his own well-being by hard work.[2] Opportunities were plentiful, and constricting rules and regulations were minimal. Enterprising businessmen could take chances without delay, and employment was continually growing, slowly in the beginning and then faster after the Korean War started in 1952.

In 1990, the situation was quite different. On one side of the former iron curtain, rich West Germans operated extremely competitive public institutions and private corporations. On the other side, poor East Germans were burdened with a noncompetitive bureaucratic system and desolate companies. Everything produced in 1949 found a buyer because the supply of goods and services was so inadequate compared with demand. In 1990, only goods that were competitive in technique, styling, and price found a buyer, because the supply of goods and services was abundant.[3]

In 1949, the bureaucracy was not a hindrance; in 1990, it was. The peaceful East German revolution of 1989 and 1990 had not destroyed the existing bureaucracy—had not even thrown out the communist officeholders. Detlev Karsten Rohwedder became chairman and chief executive officer of the Trust Company (*Treuhandgesellschaft*) in September 1990 after widespread bitter complaints about its dismal performance. He started his tenure by firing all fifteen district office heads.[4] Most of them, high officials during the communist era, had fostered mismanagement and delays through ignorance of good business practices and cronyism. Peter Christ, a reporter for the magazine *Die Zeit,* reported that West Germany had provided DM 3 billion ($1.94 billion) for immediate construction work to bolster the transition. But by August 31, two months later, government agencies had put to work only a mere DM 100 million ($64 million) of this amount.[5] Western entrepreneurs who wanted to start businesses tell horror stories about the attitudes and the ineffectiveness of the East German bureaucracy. Many early enthusiasts returned to West Germany without having been given the chance to open a branch office or a new business.

A major reason for the slow start of the free–market system in general and other bureaucratic shortcomings was the unresolved question of ownership. Under communist rule, the ownership of all "productive means" (e.g., land, buildings, factories, and even private homes) was almost totally concentrated in public hands. This concentration had to be diffused if a free–market system were to have a chance to function. However, privatization faced two major problems. Too few East Germans could afford to buy the properties and the factories from the government. Out of the understandable fear that too large a share would end up in foreign hands, the government hesitated to freely accept bids from abroad. Complicating the issue further was the fact that many of the assets had previously belonged to private citizens.[6]

Not all confiscations were regarded to be equal. Difficult discussions ensued, and complex decisions were made that were not easy to translate into effective restitution. A land reform under Soviet tutelage had taken place in East Germany between 1945 and 1949. If this reform were suddenly reversed, then 400,000 farmers and 30,000 part–time peasants (*Kleingaertner*) stood to lose their land. With Soviet support, de Maiziere, who feared allowing a precedent for other East European countries, successfully resisted the demand for restoration. But he could not prevent people whose assets were confiscated *after* 1949 from receiving the right to claim their lost properties or compensation. Some of these assets no longer existed. New houses had been built, or streets covered the ground on which they once stood. Beginning in July, the government accepted claims for restitutions; and within weeks, about a million claims were filed, many by people who lived in the West. Since many of the disputed properties were occupied by East Germans, some for as long as thirty years, resentment rose against the "rich" who came to take away the little that was left to those who stayed and suffered under communist rule. These claims created great uncertainty with regard to ownership and financial burdens.

Emergency laws were passed to make starting new businesses possible. Newly created businesses were allowed to become the owners of disputed land and property, but in such cases the purchasing price could not be finally fixed. Sellers retained the right to renegotiate the price after one year because officials believed that the initial price might not be considered a fair one in an established free–market system.

These questions were exacerbated by the bad condition of the public ownership registers. The communists had willfully neglected them in an effort to obscure the earlier private ownership.

Not only was ownership of land and properties concentrated in public hands, but the communists had also confiscated all major industries. An estimated 8,000 state–owned corporations needed to be privatized.[7] This task became the responsibility of the Trust Company (*Treuhandgesellschaft*), discussed earlier, a government agency supervised by the finance ministry in Bonn. The Trust Company's obligations were tremendous. It was to keep afloat as many corporations as possible by providing liquidity and temporary management when needed. It had to decide which corporations should be divided into smaller, more manageable units, when to introduce new accounting rules and methods, and how best to supervise the preparation of opening statements. But its most demanding task was to decide which of the 8,000 corporations could survive and which had to be closed. By one early estimate, about a quarter of them or 2,000 corporations would have to be closed because they were not competitive and had no chance of being modernized. After the Trust Company's initial failures, de Maiziere put in charge a top West German manager, the chairman of a West German steel corporation, Hoesch AG., correctly assuming that only a business leader from the West would have the experience and connections needed to administer this mammoth task.

The lack of people trained for public administration and for managing private businesses was and remains a daunting problem. To make the system work, the West German government and the private sector sent hundreds of experts over to East Germany.[8] This transfer of human capital was very important. The morning "civil servant shuttle" started from Cologne and brought several hundred top– and middle–level bureaucrats to East Germany. They returned home in the evening. Private corporations, like the big banks who opened hundreds of branch offices sometimes in construction trailers, also sent over hundreds of people. All these people came with full pay, while their East German counterparts had only about 45 percent of this amount at their disposal. The wage differential contributed to a feeling of second–class citizenship among East Germans.

It was therefore not surprising that the West German unions found eager listeners among the East German workers. The East Germans wanted to catch up with West Germany as quickly as possible. Their wages were exchanged at a 1 : 1 rate from East German Marks into DM, but their wage level was only about one–third of the West German one. Within weeks of the monetary reform, the unions succeeded in extracting double–digit wage increases and the forty-hour work week. Metal workers achieved a 26 percent increase, and the chemical workers, 35 percent.[9] Even with this round of wage negotiations, the average income of East Germany's employees reached only 45 percent of the West German level.

With wages at 45 percent of the West German level and productivity at 33 percent, prospective investors inferred correctly that East Germany would not become a low–wage country.[10] But low wages had been thought to be a major reason for investing in East Germany. Other reasons were the indigenous expertise in trade with Eastern Europe and the Soviet Union, and the expectation that investments in East Germany would be favored by tax incentives. But knowing that East Germany would not become a low–wage country, managers and entrepreneurs quickly decided that the other factors were not strong enough to force them into immediate actions. As already noted, the few positive decisions to invest in East Germany were then frustrated and delayed by bureaucratic ineptitude.

Physical obstacles to investments were also substantial—much greater than expected. It is an astonishing fact that despite the closeness of the Germanies, Westerners did not realize the degree of devastation of East Germany's environment and how serious the industrial pollution problem had become. Because West Germany was a large buyer of consumer staples, West German politicians, journalists, and business managers had regularly visited East Germany's production sites; yet, there had been almost no reports of the environmental and pollution problems. These problems seriously hampered early investment decisions.

The Schering AG, an international pharmaceutical concern, had once had their main chemical plants in East Germany but lost them because of the division of Germany. Now the East German government wanted Schering AG to buy them back. When Schering AG declined, the East German government offered the production sites for free, hoping in this way to stabilize employment. Dr. Klaus–Peter Kantzer, a member of the managing board of Schering AG, explained that his company could not accept this offer because of the unknown pollution and environmental risks.[11] In response, the East German government sweetened its offer and promised to take over the environmental risks. Schering AG had to decline again. The company feared that unknown poisonous substances hidden in the ground might pose a health hazard for employees. Schering AG preferred to build a new plant with its own money rather than to take over the one run for forty years by the East German government. The decision of Schering AG was representative of the position of many corporations. As a result, many East German plants will have to be closed down before new plants will be ready to operate. This time gap will cause unemployment.

Many well–known West German corporations (Volkswagen, Opel, Ford, Siemens, etc.) committed themselves to multi–billion dollar investments. They were convinced that East Germany would become an ideal location for production because of its talented and well–trained work force. The top managers of these corporations argued that there would not be enough space in West Germany for all industrial production needed in the future. But even in the cases in which they were prepared to use the existing East German production sites and only to retool them, an interim period without production would have to be bridged.

Professor Dr. Carl Hahn, chairman of the Volkswagen AG, encouraged other investors to regard East Germany as a premier location for new business. He argued that the productivity gap was a temporary phenomenon, caused by the lack of modern tools and management, not by the workers' unwillingness to produce.[12] But these large investments into plants and equipment require time before they can affect employment and productivity.

The architects of economic unification seriously underestimated this time gap because they thought that production would continue at the old sites until the new ones were built. But environmental concerns and lack of competitiveness closed down old East German production sites much faster than anticipated. The fate of the now-famous Trabant is a good example. Before the opening to the West, the Trabant was a popular automobile in Eastern Europe; people often spent as much as six years on a waiting list to get one. Once people in East Germany and in other Eastern countries had to pay with hard currency, this vehicle lost its attractiveness. Even a stronger, pollution–free engine manufactured by Volkswagen could not make this car competitive. Suddenly the Trabant was readily available but nobody wanted to buy it. To avoid massive layoffs before the new Volkswagen plant was ready for production, the East German government decided to subsidize the sale of this car. Ten thousand cars were sold in Eastern Europe for DM 10,000, although the production cost was DM 15,000. But other products could not be subsidized in similar ways, and employment plummeted because of lack of sales.

In the trade between communist countries, some ended the year with positive and others with negative balances. These balances were settled by transfer rubles. At the end of 1990, this practice was discontinued and the balances had to be settled with hard currencies. Since hard currencies were in very short supply in communist countries, they tried to minimize their negative balances. This hurt East Germany, because it was traditionally a large surplus country. But this was not the only reason for the sudden sharp drop in trade. Eastern Europe and the Soviet Union were in political turmoil and thus were unable to continue business as usual. Imports into this region plummeted. Since East Germany had been the main provider of industrial goods, it was hit particularly hard. Its exports plummeted literally from one day to the next and could not be replaced by orders from other countries. But this was not the only unexpected hit for East Germany's industries.

Also totally unexpected was the fact that East Germans stopped purchasing East German products. They deliberately used their DM to purchase Western goods. More than 90 percent of the detergents, cosmetics, cooking oils, and chocolate consumed in East Germany came from West Germany, and similar percentages could be named for many other products.[13] The people were simply tired of using and eating "communist products." Even East German milk and eggs were no longer accepted. In their desire to get West German goods, East Germans avoided their own retail stores and went on buying trips to West Germany. Almost every fourth East German, exactly 22 percent of them, bought a new car after July 2. But they bought a Western car.[14] The flip side of this development was that West Germany's producers and retailers had their best year in history.

By September 1990 the architects of the economic unification should have noticed that their model was not working. But political expediency did not allow them to admit failure; so they lost valuable time for adjustments. All sectors of the economy—farming, industry, retailing—shrank, and no indices pointed to a recovery. In 1990, East Germany lost 1.5 million jobs.[15] Not all of these people became unemployed however. About 100,000 East Berliners found employment in West Berlin, and another 200,000 East Germans began to leave their homes every morning to commute to work in West Germany. Nevertheless, about 27 percent of the total work force was either unemployed or on short work at the end of December.[16] The following figures show how serious the deterioration really was:

Germany's Economic Performance in 1990[17] (in Percent)

	West	East
GNP Growth (nominal)	8.2	-18.5
GNP Growth (real)	4.6	-13.5
Investments in Equipment	13.6	-14.5
Investments in Plants	11.4	- 7.0
Exports	10.3	8.0
Imports	10.1	57.5

These figures indicate a serious breakdown in economic activity. But the East Germans did not fully feel the impact, for it was cushioned by a strong social net that prevented individuals from falling into financial deprivation. Officials in the East and West also tried to uphold the public spirit by stressing the temporary nature of this downturn.

Anxiety rose again during the summer months. Even the flight to the West resumed.[18] The East Germans demanded that their interim government should end the negotiations with West Germany so that the political unification could also occur. These people believed that the turn for the better would come only when a single government would rule over all of Germany. The East German politicians were

heavily influenced by these demands; and on June 17, a "wild unification" almost happened. On this memorial day for the 1953 uprising of
workers in East Berlin, the deputies of the DSU tried to convince the
East German parliament to vote for an immediate merger with West
Germany. De Maiziere had great difficulties preventing this from
happening. The situation remained tense, and there was no doubt
that the slightest disappointment in the further negotiations about
the political unification would trigger another effort for an immediate
merger.

In summary, the economic development after the introduction
of the DM was a major disappointment for both the people and the
responsible officials. It did not bring the expected relief. After a very
short period of time, stress and anxieties rose again. The partici-
pants of the two–plus–four negotiations realized that the negotiations
needed to come to an end if a wild unification should be prevented.
The East Germans continued to exert pressure that could not be ig-
nored in the capitals of the world. They continued to be the driving
force behind the unification.

E. The Political Unification of Germany

The completion of the first stage of unification on July 2, 1990, was, however sweeping (it resolved the major economic, social, and monetary issues), nevertheless only the *first* major step. The second brought political unification. The decision to divide the process into these two steps was made to gain time so negotiations of the international aspects of the unification could occur in an orderly fashion.[1] The East German people had elected an interim parliament and government solely to negotiate and execute the unification with West Germany. Lothar de Maiziere was well aware of this fact and therefore put together a government consisting of all major democratic parties. It was an oversized government—that means, its parliamentary base was larger than 51 percent.

It was not easy to put together such a large coalition government consisting of the CDU, DSU, F.D.P., and SPD. The election campaign had left some hard feelings behind, in particular among SPD members. Moreover, important ideological differences existed between the CDU, DSU, and F.D.P. on one hand, and the SPD on the other.[2] But eventually the differences were overcome, and the East German politicians realized that they needed to unite for the upcoming negotiations with the West German delegation which, on their side, started in a much stronger position.

The de Maiziere government was often called an "amateur government" because none of its members had prior experience in government or any knowledge about democratic procedures.[3] Even so, it earned great respect for the professional way in which it approached the difficult task at hand. De Maiziere himself made it his obligation to negotiate for a fair compromise. His CDU background and his unassuming manner significantly helped him gain more than one important concession.

The international roadblocks to unification were finally removed by Gorbachev and Kohl in Stravopol in July 1990.[4] Now the so-called "Unification Treaty" (*Einigungsvertrag*) between the two German states had to be finalized. By early summer, it was widely assumed that the unification would occur shortly before or after the West German election on December 2, 1990. But the conditions in East Germany deteriorated so rapidly that an earlier date needed to be found. East Germany was simply no longer a viable political and economic entity. With very few exceptions, East Germans wanted the interim status to end as soon as possible.[5] The earliest date that could be realistically chosen was the third of October. This was only two days after the important CSCE conference in New York where the "Treaty on the Final Settlement With Respect to Germany" was presented.

The first item on the internal German negotiation table was the electoral law intended to direct the first all–German election. Existing West German law prevented small parties (those with less than 5 percent of the total vote) from sending deputies into parliament. De Maiziere argued that East Germany needed a different rule, for a number of small East German parties had contributed so much to the revolution that they deserved a chance to enter the first democratically elected all–German parliament. De Maiziere requested either a lower threshold, perhaps 3 percent instead of 5 percent, or that the 5 percent minimum be applied state by state, not country wide.[6]

This issue divided the East German government. The SPD regarded it as a ploy to help the small DSU survive and to split the left. It was generally believed that the DSU and the PDS would benefit the most by a change of the minimum rule. The SPD regarded the DSU as a right–wing party and the PDS as its main competitor on the left and had no interest in fostering their survival. The debate grew very emotional. On July 25, the F.D.P. was the first party to leave the de Maiziere coalition. The SPD followed a few weeks later. These departures did not, however, bring down the de Maiziere government. De Maiziere continued to rule, even with only a minority in parliament, because the opposition could not gather a majority without including the PDS, and such a coalition was politically impossible.

The fight over the electoral law caused a marked deterioration of public trust in the elected officials. The East Germans could not understand why their elected representatives played such trivial political games while the country went to pieces economically. Once again, the East German people became restive. They demanded an end to the transition period.

The controversy spilled over into West Germany's party politics.

There the F.D.P., itself a small party, opposed all efforts to make the entrance into parliament easier for small parties. The F.D.P. feared that its own constituency would splinter. Suddenly the F.D.P. and the SPD were on the same side of an argument against the CDU/CSU. Before this escalated into a coalition crisis, the F.D.P., the coalition partner of the CDU/CSU, suggested a compromise that was accepted by the main West German parties. But now the PDS saw only disadvantages for itself and filed suit in Germany's federal court. The federal court struck down the compromise and more or less dictated a solution. The coalition drafted a new law based on the court's proposal, and the Bundestag and Bundesrat passed it into law. With that the last hurdle was taken just in time so that the united Germany could vote for a new parliament.

According to the final law, the 5 percent hurdle was applied separately to East and West Germany in the upcoming election. This meant that parties in East Germany needed a minimum of 600,000 votes to send a deputy into the parliament, while in West Germany 2,250,000 votes were needed to pass the threshold. The law also allowed election alliances among East German parties, giving them an additional way to pass the 5 percent hurdle. The court also stipulated that the law had to be changed before the next federal election.

Another issue drew much public attention: should Berlin immediately become the capital of the united Germany? Both the public and politicians were split about this issue. Finally, Berlin was chosen as the capital of Germany.[8] However, the parliament and the government will remain in Bonn for the time being. As a result, Berlin is the titular capital and the location of some government agencies, while Bonn remains the political center. Many people believe that this decision will be revised later.

Four major considerations contributed to this decision. First, after the fall of the Kaiserreich in 1918, the newly elected democratic government was forced to flee from Berlin to Weimar. Daily demonstrations made the orderly functioning of government impossible. Since Berlin again became the center of both leftist and rightist demonstrations, those historical memories played a role. Second, the government in 1990 wanted to avoid any association with the "Reich." Chancellor Kohl wanted to demonstrate that the unified Germany should not be regarded as the "Fourth Reich." Bonn, a small university city, will not compete with Paris or London for grandeur and splendor. Third, cost considerations were also important. The move of parliament and government to Berlin was estimated to cost DM 20 billion ($13 billion). In addition to Berlin's famous Reichstag building, to house the government, other offices and many private homes would have had to be built before the government could consider moving to the undivided Berlin. Fourth, Catholic Southern German states did not want to move the government back to the Protestant North of the country.

If a single political issue consumed most of the public attention, it was abortion.[9] Under the influence of conservatives, West Germany had outlawed abortion in 1975, allowing it only in special cases such as when the mother's life was at risk. Women's groups and leftist parties never stopped agitating against this law. In East Germany, by contrast, abortion was generally permitted. Most East Germans believed in a mother's right to decide whether she wants to continue a pregnancy. After endless debates, an agreement was reached involving a two–year transition period. During these two years, East and West Germany agreed to have different laws. Then, the emerging parliament will have the task of deciding the issue for the unified Germany.

The unification treaty also answered many other transitional problems.[10] That treaty will influence developments for years after the transition period comes to its scheduled end in 1994. The main goal is eventually to unify all laws and regulations and to contribute to equalizing the living conditions in both regions. But laws and regulations can only provide a framework that must be filled in by private initiatives.

At midnight on October 2, 1990, the local copy of Philadelphia's Liberty Bell rang for the new beginning in freedom and unity. In a Bundestag address in Berlin on October 3, 1990, President Weizsaecker expressed the feelings of many Germans:

> . . . Now we have a state that we no longer regard as temporary and whose identity and integrity are no longer questioned by its neighbors. On this very day, the united German nations is finding an accepted place in Europe.

> . . . For the Germans in East Germany the unification is a daily and very personal process of change. This often presents superhuman challenges. A woman wrote to me that she was deeply grateful for the freedom but that she did not know beforehand how much burden these changes

would become and that it would be a real farewell to the old existence. Her greatest wish had been to get rid of the old regime. But she had not known that with that, all elements of her life would be replaced by something new from one day to the next.[11]

Fireworks rocketed above the Brandenburg Gate and elsewhere in the country, but everywhere the happy mood was mixed with anxiety. The Allensbach Institute that closely studied the mood of the people had found that during 1990 in East and West Germany, more and more people regarded the unification as a favorable event.[12] The positive support grew to 75 percent in West Germany and remained over 80 percent in East Germany, despite the disappointing ecomomic developments during the summer months. But Allensbach also revealed substantial differences of opinion with regard to financial support and solidarity. Most West Germans, 55 percent to be exact, argued that they had worked hard for their high living standard and expected the East Germans to do likewise. They felt that East Germans should not demand sharing or hand-outs but should accept that they were economically behind and work hard to catch up. But 78 percent of the East Germans believed that it was not their fault that they were behind. They believed that political circumstances beyond their control had robbed them of forty years of positive development. Now the West Germans, so fortunate to be on the "right" side of the iron curtain, had, in East German eyes, the moral obligation to show solidarity and to provide the means needed to raise rapidly the living conditions in the Eastern part of the common fatherland. Those polls demonstrated that formal unification may have been achieved in the morning hours of the third of October but that human unification had a long way to go.[13]

IV. IN THE AFTERMATH OF THE UNIFICATION

A. The State Election in East Germany and the Federal Election in Germany as a Whole

The German people had reached their goal. They lived in a single state that had gained full sovereignty. But much had to be accomplished internally before an orderly democratic process was well established.

The West German Constitution, now governing Germany as a whole, required that Germany be organized as a federal state. After World War II in West Germany, twelve states had reemerged. Then three small states merged to form Baden–Wuerttemberg. And in 1957, the Saarland voted to join the federation. Thus, there were finally ten West German states. The communists had centralized East Germany. Now the individual states within it had to be resurrected. East Germany historically had consisted of five states. The communist centralization was unable to destroy the regional diversities, and thus the same five states reappeared. The final step of this process was the state election on October 14, 1990.

West Berlin and East Berlin were slated to merge and to form the sixteenth state of the German federation. Since this merger was expected to happen between October and December 1990, the election of the new state parliament was postponed to December 2, 1990.

The German states were different in size and population:

The Size of the Population in German States[1]
(in Millions)

West German States

North Rhine–Westfalia	16.7
Bavaria	10.9
Baden–Wuerttemberg	9.3
Lower Saxony	7.2

Hesse	5.5
Rhineland–Palatinate	3.6
Schleswig–Holstein	2.6
Hamburg	1.6
Saarland	1.1
Bremen	.7

East German States

Saxony	4.9
Saxony–Anhalt	3.0
Brandenburg	2.7
Thuringia	2.5
Mecklenburg	2.3

East and West Berlin   3.2

Experts argued that sixteen states were too many and inefficient to administer and suggested numerous plans to consolidate the German federal structure.[2] But all those efforts failed because regional and ethnic differences were still remarkably strong. People also wanted their governments close at hand and not in a distant capital.

In this state election in October 1990, the third within a year in East Germany, the CDU was the big winner, taking 54.9 percent of the total votes and, more importantly, the majority in four out of five states.

Elections in the Five East German States[3]
October 14, 1990
(in percent)

	CDU	FDP	SPD	PDS	Small P.*
Mecklenburg	38.3	5.5	27.0	15.7	13.5
Brandenburg	29.4	6.6	38.3	13.4	12.3
Saxony–Anhalt	39.0	13.5	26.0	12.0	9.5
Saxony	53.8	5.3	19.1	10.2	11.6
Thuringia	45.4	9.3	22.8	9.7	12.8

*Small parties: The most important small parties are Buendnis 90 and The Greens.

Most East Germans voted in this election, as in the previous two, for parties who had worked for the unification despite the economic woes that accompanied it. The CDU was able to gain a strong foothold among workers, the usual stronghold of the SPD. The F.D.P. improved its position and clearly benefited from Genscher's popularity. In Genscher's home state, Saxony–Anhalt, the F.D.P. reached a double digit–result. The SPD was again disappointed. It became the largest party in only one state, Brandenburg, and there gained the office of the minister–president. The decline of the PDS continued, although a hard core of supporters, around 10 percent of the votes, seemed to exist.

The political and economic reconstruction of East Germany was supported by many West Germans who left their comfortable lives, settled in East Germany, and started to work for democratization. Rudi Arndt—"Red Rudi," the former lord–mayor of Frankfurt—went to Erfurt. Hinrich Lehmann–Grube, the city–manager of Hannover, was elected as lord–mayor of Leipzig. Heinz Remmers, former minister of Lower Saxony, moved to Saxony–Anhalt and became minister of justice. However, the most prominent transferee was Professor Kurt Biedenkopf.[4] He was a CDU heavyweight before a controversy with Helmut Kohl temporarily interrupted his political career. Early in 1990, he moved from a teaching position in Muenster to the University of Leipzig where teachers trained in the West were desperately needed. From there, he organized the CDU election campaign and won a decisive victory in a historic stronghold of the SPD. These moves by prominent people to East Germany were very influential. These individuals brought with them great administrative and political experience. Even more important were their connections to the political machinery in West Germany and to the press. They had the credibility that many East German politicians lacked. Their statements were taken as fair and measured and influenced West German public opinion.

On October third, the East German parliament was dissolved. One hundred forty–four East German deputies became members of the parliament in Bonn which, from that day on, was responsible for Germany as a whole. This brief transitional period came to an end on December 2, 1990, when all eligible Germans went to the polls.

The federal election on December 2, 1990, ended the unification process that had started on November 9, 1989, when the Berlin Wall crumbled and the first banners in East Germany appeared affirming that there was only one German people and one Germany. This election also gave the German people the opportunity to express their judgments about the different approaches to the question of unification chosen by the various parties and their leading representatives.

In this election, parties that had not univocally supported an early unification lost in a big way. The SPD had its worst showing since 1957, with only one-third of the total votes. The West German Greens did not ever reach the minimum necessary to return to the Bundestag. Only the East German Greens (Gruene/Buendnis 90) passed the 5 percent hurdle—with 6.1 percent of the votes in East Germany—and could therefore send two deputies to the Bundestag.[5] Together, conservative parties gained 54.8 percent of the votes, the expected comfortable majority in parliament and the right to form the next governnemt.

The Outcome of the Federal Election of December 2, 1990[6]

	West Germany	East Germany	Total
CDU/CSU	44.3	41.8	43.8
F.D.P.	10.6	12.9	11.0
SPD	35.7	24.3	33.5
Greens	4.8	6.1	5.1
PDS	.3	11.1	2.4
Other Parties	4.3	3.8	4.2
	100.0	100.0	100.0

Fewer people than usual went to ballot boxes. Only 77.8 percent of the eligible voters participated, compared with 84.4 percent in the 1987 West German election and 99.3 percent in the East German election on March 18. There were several reasons for this low participation, measured against normal German standards. In East Germany, this was the fourth election within one year; people were tired of going to the ballot boxes. Only the supporters of the PDS showed the discipline to vote in large numbers. In West Germany, conservatives were convinced that their parties would win by a wide margin and stayed home. Because they expected a defeat, SPD voters did so also. Many supporters of The Greens did not vote because they were angry about the infighting within their own party.[7]

In October and November, many observers had feared that the CDU/CSU would gain an absolute majority and thus would be able to form the government alone—a result the F.D.P. would have considered a catastrophe and one that would have been, in a sense, unjust, since this party had in Hans–Dietrich Genscher one of the architects of the unification. Therefore, the F.D.P. campaign was directed foremost against the absolute majority of its coalition partner, not against the other competition. This factor was detrimental to the bourgeois camp. But Helmut Kohl was at the peak of his popularity, and Genscher was expected to attract some additional votes for his party. Therefore, people expected a very strong showing of both bourgeois parties despite the divisiveness of their election campaigns. Oskar Lafontaine's campaign rallies were attended more for the entertainment value than for the appeal of his political message. The West German Greens had entered the final stage of a battle on basic positions between their fundamentalist and pragmatic wings and thus robbed themselves of all chances to be a factor in this election.

In all of Germany, the CDU/CSU got only 43.8 percent of the votes, their lowest share since 1969. Back in 1983, when Kohl had toppled Helmut Schmidt, 48.8 percent had voted for him and the CDU/CSU. Even in the uneventful election of 1987, 44.3 percent voted for the Christian Democrats. The 43.8 percent figures was a big disappointment for Helmut Kohl and his party. Three explanations were presented:

1. Gary Geipel argued:

> The conservative victory in Germany was a triumph of demographics, not of reunification. If Germany's 18- to 45-year-olds had decided the election alone, an SPD–The Greens Party coalition, under the chancellor candidate Oskar Lafontaine, would have won.[8]

Geipel continued that the conservative voter base was dying out and that this was the last election that the conservatives would win easily if the CDU/CSU continued to fail to attract new, young voters. The SPD used this argument for consolation. However, a closer look revealed that only a majority of the age cohorts between 25 and 45 voted for the SPD and The Greens. Most of the youngest voters, those between 18 and 24, voted conservative.[9]

2. A second widely published explanation postulated that this election demonstrated the general support for Kohl's concept but also the fear of many people about the financial consequences of unification. This duality of feelings, which made many bourgeois voters stay home, was thus responsible for the dismal showing by the CDU/CSU. This explanation was based on impressions but not on hard data.

3. Finally, the argument was made that both mass parties, the CDU/CSU as well as the SPD, had lost the ability to control the political process in Germany. This argument is based on thoughtful research and deserves further explanation.

Historically, the CDU/CSU and SPD, the two mass parties, usually gained about 90 percent of the votes, relegating the other parties to a marginal existence. One of the two mass parties was able to attract the small F.D.P. and thus form a majority government. But in the last two decades, party loyalty declined, as did the attractiveness and membership in party–support organizations.

Neither the CDU/CSU nor the SPD can hope to ever win an absolute majority in the future nor can both together expect to control the political process in the way they have. Their combined share of the votes declined to under 80 percent, giving the smaller parties a stronger voter base and more importance. Many political analysts believe that this decline is irreversible. They argue that the voter has become increasingly independent and that the assumed variety of political needs can no longer be provided by two mass parties alone. Other parties were needed and have filled the gaps. They are here to stay.

The SPD will have to share the votes which are left of the center with one, or perhaps two, other parties (The Greens and the PDS); and the CDU/CSU will have to cope with a stronger F.D.P. and perhaps also with a party oriented further to the right (The Republicans).[10]

The decline of the two mass parties started in the late seventies when the issues of peace, environment, and feminism did not find enough resonance in the existing parties. Since then, other issues (fear of influx of too may foreigners, and, simultaneously, a stronger national feeling) led to the formation of this new rightist party, The Republicans. Kohl's bold moves toward unification took much wind out of their sails, with the result that The Republicans did not enter the Bundestag. However, in Bavaria they remain an important factor, reducing the weight of the Christian party. During the time of issue proliferation, the once-predictable loyalty between party sympathizers and party weakened. The number of so-called independent voters increased to the point that Professor Noelle–Neumann estimated that about one-third of the electorate described itself as independent, not led by a particular party. She argued that no reversal of either trend is in sight. That Helmut Kohl, even at the peak of his popularity, could not break or interrupt this trend was taken as strong confirmation that Germany has moved from a two-and-one-half party system to a moderate multi-party system, meaning a party system with four to five parties.

A major result of this election was that only the CDU/CSU was able to form a majority government. A coalition between the SPD, The Greens, and the F.D.P. would have fallen short of a majority; and the inclusion of the PDS was politically impossible. If the election is viewed in this way, the CDU/CSU gained a profound victory and put its arch rival, the SPD, into a decidedly secondary position where it is likely to remain as long as it cannot present a credible alternative to the CDU/CSU as a party able to build a coalition. The F.D.P., even if it wanted, could not contemplate coalescing with any party other than the CDU/CSU, so there simply was no viable alternative to a CDU/CSU–F.D.P. coalition.

The successor to the communist party, the PDS, received 11.1 percent in East Germany and .3 percent in West Germany. As expected, the PDS could not gain a foothold in West Germany and even lost votes in East Germany, compared with the May 18 election, where it had gained 16.3 percent of the votes. However, the 11.1 percent is still a remarkable result especially since the reputation of the PDS was shattered by financial scandals before the election. One must conclude that the PDS still has a loyal, hard core following. Party leader Gysi won 31.8 percent of the first votes in his Berlin district and thus a direct mandate for the Bundestag. This result was one more sign that the communist past had not been fully overcome and that Minister–President Biedenkopf's warnings about the continuing efforts of former communists to get a foothold in the new administration were not exaggerated.

In the summer of 1988, public opinion had turned against Chancellor Kohl. *Die Zeit* and other important publications suggested that Kohl should abdicate, to give a fresh face to shine—or else, the CDU/CSU would certainly lose the 1990 election.[11] Resistance to Kohl's chancellorship developed within the party. He skillfully weathered the storm in 1988, and in 1989 his fortunes started to turn when he realized earlier than all other leading Western politicians that, first, public opinion would swing towards unification and, second, the international circumstances were such that unification was possible. In retrospect, it can be justly said that without Chancellor Kohl, unification would not have happened in the way and at the time it actually did. Subsequent events in the Soviet Union make it certain that had Kohl not achieved unification when he did, the final merger of the two Germanies would have been delayed for years.

In a very personal sense, Kohl was rewarded for all of his efforts. Throughout his political career, he campaigned in a staunch SPD district. At the center of his Ludwigshafen district was the chemical concern, BASF (Badische Anilin und Soda Fabrik), with tens of thousands of workers who voted for the SPD for generations. But in 1990, Helmut Kohl beat his SPD opponent and won the direct mandate for the Bundestag for the first time.

Together with the federal election, Berlin elected its state parliament. In a surprise outcome, the CDU/CSU emerged as the strongest party, relegating the SPD to the second place. This was another triumph for the CDU/CSU and was generally interpreted as a special reward for the unification efforts.[12]

The outcome of the elections on December 2, 1990, were determined by the unification process and rewarded Kohl and Genscher and their parties for their achievements. However, that the reward was smaller than expected, in particular for the CDU/CSU, foreshadowed the difficulties the new government was to confront. After political unification was achieved, the task still remained to unite the East and West German people emotionally, socially, and economically.

B. The Communist Heritage and the Legacy It Left Behind

The communists ruled East Germany from 1945 to 1990. Many people born during this period had never experienced any other way of life. It was about 1980 when unbiased information via West German TV began to penetrate the iron curtain. Thus, East Germans had learned to think and act differently than people brought up under different circumstances. This was one of the legacies the communist system left behind. Another was that communist cadres tried to preserve themselves and influential positions in the new democratic era, often building a layer of resistance to the new order. Since many former communists—members of the hated secret police in particular—are not known by the public, distrust of officials and bureaucrats is rampant. The third legacy is that even opponents of the former communist system do not believe that the democratic/capitalist system of West Germany is the best system available; they still believe that a merger of the good traits of both system would have been much more appealing.

These differences, originating in the upbringing under communist rule, hinder the parts of Germany from growing together rapidly. Now doubts about unification are heightened by the economic depression that hit the East Germans so unexpectedly. But the communist heritage is a burden for both Germanies, and much empathy on both sides will be needed to overcome the cleavage that it left behind.

A communist system is a totalitarian system, and East German communism was no exception. There the party members tried to penetrate every sphere of life and to keep all people permanently involved and motivated in their communist agenda. No private sphere in contrast with a public sphere existed. One's education, job, promotions, housing, and success in general depended on whether one seemed to support the communist cause or not. Not everyone had to be a member of the communist party, although 2.3 million people of the 12 million adults were.[1] For most lower–level and middle–class people, it was sufficient to be a *Mitlaeufer*—that is, a person who neither supported nor opposed the system but who was always willing to participate in the required meetings and functions. To belong to the highest stratum of the society, party membership and appearance of active cooperation were essential.

The state had deeply infiltrated all segments of life. The state security apparatus (*Stasi* or the *Staatssicherheitsdienst*) had about 85,000 employees, 45,000 high-level functionaries, and 500,000 informants.[2] On the average, one informant covered 330 people. Lawyers (like Wolfgang Schnur or Lothar de Maiziere) who wanted a favorable verdict for a client were forced to render "services" in return. Middle-class parents who were known not to be active supporters of the regime were often forced to render services so that their children might be allowed to enter a high school and therefore not deprived of an education. Between rulers and ruled, and between people who took advantage and those who were victims of the regime, the lines were frequently blurred.

Most people did not feel that the communist regime was oppressive and were not in open or hidden opposition all the time. In fact, there was only one revolt in the forty-five years of communist rule.[3] The regime and the people had reached an accommodation with each other, in which the regime was not threatened and the people enjoyed a poor but generally predictable life. If a citizen did not threaten the regime and rendered the services requested from him, then he knew that he would have a predetermined job and career without having to fear unemployment or poverty. The regime knew that it had to provide a slowly rising living standard that compared well with the other communist states.

Many East Germans had relatives in West Germany. The family of Lothar de Maiziere is an excellent example.[4] The other branch of this family lived in West Germany; indeed, one of them was a general in the West German air force. East and West Germans always wanted to have the right and possibility to visit in both countries. As a result, in the last ten years, people increasingly had the chance to compare their living standard with the one in Western societies. The discrepancy between them added tremendously to the East German sense of isolation. The demand for free travel became a unifying request, one whose explosive power the regime totally underestimated.[5]

It is important to realize that in the fall of 1989 the reform movement neither wanted to remove the communist regime nor to give up the existence of the East German state. The leaders of this peaceful reform movement wanted only to open the regime and the borders of the country. They wanted to share power; and the "round table," if properly handled, would have fulfilled many of their requests. These reform leaders stood for "democratic or humane socialism," and they believed that the "real socialism" of East Germany could be peacefully transformed.[6] They believed a third alternative lay somewhere in the middle between socialism and capitalism and wanted East Germany to become a model for this "third way." For them, the social component of the system should not be limited to the bargaining process between management and labor but should deeply penetrate the production process by co–determination and co–decision making about investments, plant openings, and similar issues. The goals of the society they envisioned were a healthy environment, equality of people (as far as possible), and an increased living standard. The reformer's goal of equality entailed a much more democratic form of government than the communists provided, but was simultaneously opposed to what they perceived to be the interest group–driven form of Western democracy. This model had many supporters among the intellectual elite. Even Oskar Lafontaine, the outspoken chancellor candidate of the West German SPD, supported it.

The "third way" also attracted a great deal of public support. The demonstrations in October demanded a dual opening—the opening of the government for other than communist forces and the opening of the border to the West. But by not acting quickly and decisively, the communists wasted their chance to attack the public demonstrations. The regime lost control of the media; and, in turn, the media started to learn about and publicize the privileges and corruption inside the ruling class. The media revelations shocked the East Germans who had truly believed that their leaders shared, albeit to a lesser extent, their own misery. A feeling of betrayal crept into their minds and ruined their confidence that this state was worth the effort of being transformed and rescued. This profound change in public opinion occurred virtually overnight. It put an end not only to the communist rule but also to the chances for an independent, humane, socialistic state on East Germany's soil. It did *not*, however, destroy the dream that such a state and such a society were goals worth fighting for. The public began to believe that their ideal state would have to be built in a much larger and much more diversified environment, in the reunited Germany. Unification did not end their dream that a democratic–socialist state should and could be the final result of all political and educational efforts. This credo survived the process of unification. An influential group of people continued, and continues, to believe that the democratic/capitalistic system is only the second best possible one.

The unification occurred on West Germany's terms. East Germany gave up its identity and its former way of life to adopt the West German ways. For some people, this change felt like having lost a war. The victors came and brought with them their institutions, their laws, and their ideas about how things should be done. For most East Germans, a rapid learning process began. They had to learn what a democracy and a competitive economic system really meant and how one had to behave in order to survive and progress in it. Some East Germans complained that not much really changed.[7] Before unification, they stood in line for consumer goods; after unification, they stand in line for tax and social security formulas.

Women especially complained that they were victimized by unification. One of East Germany's social accomplishments was the availability of free kindergarten for everyone. This enabled women to participate in the work force in higher numbers than in many West European societies. Now their "liberation" from the home seemed threatened because the democratic/capitalistic system was unable to provide kindergarten free of charge. The immediate increase in unemployment hit women even harder than men and contributed to this feeling of a great loss.

The deteriorating economic situation further increased the anxieties among East Germans. At the end of 1991, one year after unification, about one–third of the East German work force was either unemployed or on short work, and discouraged to know that it would get worse before it could get better. Despite the high compensations for unemployment and short work, the mood was depressed.

The cooperation between experts from West Germany and people from the East did not go as well as hoped. West German experts were usually in leading positions and were supposed to teach their East German employees. Tensions were unavoidable, heightened by the fact that the West Germans worked for much higher wages than their East German counterparts. More than once, one heard East Germans say that they felt as if they had lost a war and that an occupation force was trying to install a new system. Those feelings became even more exacerbated when the East Germans realized that most of the production they lost went to West Germany. After unification, West Germans enjoyed one of their most prosperous years in recent history. Boom in the West and depression in the East, high wages in the West and low ones in the East, knowledge about how to do things correctly in one area and the need to learn the capitalistic ways in the other— these and more problems contributed to the feeling that a two–class society had come into being.

At the end of 1990, the mood was a mixture of hope that the promised good times would arrive in spring, fear that these good times would never come, and the rising feeling that something of value was lost without having been replaced by a better value. Optimism, resignation, and disappointment resided closely together.

In January of 1991, the original joy over the unification was like a distant dream. East and West Germans had increasing difficulties communicating with each other. The rising demands for financial support from the five new states were met with growing impatience and unwillingness in West Germany. In East Germany, disappointment about the lack of solidarity and empathy spread. On the individual level, people had difficulties talking with each other and finding a common ground for discussions.[8]

Based on thorough opinion research, Professor Helmut Klages argued that this development had to be expected and was not surprising at all.[9] In Klages' opinion, the misunderstandings were caused by sharply differing value systems in East and West Germany and exacerbated by the economic disparity of boom in the West and depression in the East.

After the war, the value systems in East and West Germany were similar. Both were based on the protestant ethic and led to a relatively better performance of both Germanies in relation to their neighbors. West Germany grew faster than France and Britain; East Germany became the industrial powerhouse of the communist bloc. But there the similarities ended. In East Germany, the communists tried to destroy the milieu of petty bourgeois values and replace it with obedience and conformism. Obedience, not leadership, was rewarded. Over time people became content to follow orders instead of developing their own intiatives. West German developments went in the opposite direction. The value revolution of the late sixties put the goal of self–realization at the center of all efforts, meaning that the individual tried to be more self–directed and self–centered than before. This in turn increased individual initiatives and reduced the sense of solidarity. Based on this analysis, it is not surprising that West Germans are puzzled about the lack of self–reliance and personal initiatives of many East Germans. The East Germans in turn are deeply troubled about the lack of Western solidarity.

Klages argued that the present economic disparity, if not soon overcome, could inflict permanent damage on the relationship of the two parts of Germany. In West Germany, a sense of superiority may take hold, while in East Germany many people might settle for a substandard life without the drive for improvement. Even today, some people can be found who are becoming comfortable with their unemployment status. If opportunities do not open up fairly soon, then permanent damage has to be expected.

The sudden clash of the two civilizations is not the only problem confronting the East and West Germans. The revolution in East Germany occurred in a peaceful manner. This had great advantages for the society at large but also gave the communist cadres ample time to prepare themselves for survival under the new, democratic leadership. The communists managed the transition so successfully that Fritz Ullrich Fack, an influential West German commentator, argued that the communists had become an important part of the new ruling class.[10] The Modrow government, for example, gave many people the chance to look through their personal files and to "correct" them. This allowed many second–tier communists to cover their tracks and to survive in their positions.[11] Through the existing network, other former communists were placed into lucrative positions. This consolidation continued during the rule of de Maiziere. His Minister of the Interior, Distel, wanted to avoid prosecution of communists. He believed that East Germany should not be split into two classes of people, one being the former communists and the other being the former "Mitlaeufer." But Distel went too far with appeasement. Resistance groups developed inside the public administration. Hans Rohwedder, the "imported" boss of the Trust Company, was convinced that the dismal performance of his agency could be blamed partially on the resistance of former communist officials. He fired all of them.[12]

The East Germans were less forgiving than their Minister of the Interior. They had not forgotten the atrocities of the secret police and wanted every member of this unit to be removed from public life. To be accused of being a former "Stasi" was almost enough to discredit a person completely. The first victims were the new leaders of the newly formed democratic parties. Wolfgang Schnur, the leader of the Awakening Party, was a lawyer who had successfully defended dissidents against the communist regime, and by doing so, he had come into contact with the hated secret police.[13] He resigned shortly before the March election. Ibrahim Boehme, the flamboyant leader of the SPD, was so deeply hurt by these accusations that he attempted suicide. Months later, his name was cleared. Lothar de Maiziere was able to defend himself successfully against similar accusations for half a year. But in December of 1990, the grounds for suspicion became so overwhelming that he resigned from his political positions. Later his name was cleared and he resumed his political duties, but a shadow of distrust remained. How delicate the situation really was can be shown by the example of Ralf Hirsch, an East German assistant of West Berlin's Lord–Mayor Momper who was accused of having worked for the secret police.[14] Hirsch, in his early forties, found out that the secret police had amassed sixteen volumes, each about two inches thick, of information about him. These volumes contained, among other things, detailed accounts about his most private life. At Hirsch's expense, eight lawyers sifted through the documents and fortunately for him found a statement characterizing him as "very uncooperative." The latest entries were made as late as February 1990, a clear indication that the secret police continued their work through the transition period.

The main communist vehicle for survival in the democratic era became the successor of the communist party, the PDS. Gregor Gysi, the newly elected party chairman, refused to sever the ties with the old communist party.[15] The PDS became the successor party of the SED and thus inherited all its wealth. Once the SED had accurately boasted that it was the richest party in the world: after a scandal, DM 107 million ($69 million) were secretly and illegally transferred to bank accounts abroad, and Gysi admitted as late as November 4, 1990, that the possessions of the party surpassed DM 2.2 billion ($1.42 billion).[16] Other dealings also comprised the PDS and left no doubt about its intent to protect and support former communists. The secret service is said to have transferred its wealth to the PDS.[17] The PDS was also forced to admit having given low interest rate loans to former communists and communist–run enterprises.[18] The widespread suspicion that the former communists were able to build a secret network of relationships is partially real and partially imagined, but it will certainly damage the social fabric for some time to come. Minister–President Biedenkopf summarized these problems in the following way:

> Besides the physical devastation of the country, the main malaise is the stultification of the people's imagination. This is particularly prevalent in the fact that people had not learned to take responsibilities. The number of candidates for new leadership positions is very small. And one also has to compete with West German states, being able to pay salaries only half as big as the Western competitor.[19]

Political unification was achieved on the third of October, 1990, but social unification will take some time to emerge. The East Germans cannot simply undo within one year what the communist rule has done in forty–five years. Communists, often unrecognized, are still a problem, sometimes real but more often imagined. The economic depression made all these problems much more severe. But even if the economic tide would turn soon, the problem of growing together socially will remain.[20]

C. The Economic Outlook for East Germany

Politicians frequently lament that there is no economic theory for the transformation of a planned into a free–market economy. This accusation is both true and false. It is true that there is no cookbook–like prescription for such a transformation, because every case has its idiosyncracies stemming from the history and the level of development of the country in question. But there is a great body of knowledge about some fundamental facts that are similar in many such transitions.

The economists—for example, Karl–Otto Poehl, the president of the Deutsche Bundesbank—had warned that the sudden transformation of the East German economy from a controlled one to a free one is an extremely costly enterprise. Helmut Kohl made the political decision to do it anyway because he believed that the then–existing favorable international political climate had to be used to break East Germany away from the Soviet hemisphere.

East Germany was comparable to other countries with which the International Monetary Fund (IMF) had dealt earlier. It was comparable to developing countries that wanted to open themselves to the global economy. In all of those cases, the IMF had requested that the opening of the domestic market in the developing country should be accompanied by large investments and by a drastic devaluation of its currency.[1] Immediate large–scale investments were supposed to create new jobs and thus compensate for those that might be lost in industries that became noncompetitive through this drastic change in economic policy. The currency devaluation was included in order to make indigenous production more competitive on world markets and to increase the prices of imported products that competed with the domestically produced items. Both measures were designed to help the "opened" economy over the initial shock of international competition.

In East Germany, however, the opening of the domestic market to the forces of international competition was accompanied by a dramatic increase in the value of its new currency and by a lack of sudden new investments. The currency exchange occurred at the most favorable rate of 1 : 1 for the larger part of the private savings and, more important here, for wages and other forms of income. On top of that, immediately after the currency reform, the work force asked for and received a wage increase of roughly 40 percent. The currency exchange and the following wage increases resulted in an overvaluation of the currency. This overvaluation can best be demonstrated by a comparison of two indices. The East German labor force received compensation that amounted to 45 percent of the West German level. But the productivity was only 33 percent of West Germany's one. The outcome was that East Germany had an expensive labor force, if one correctly assumes that productivity cannot be increased overnight. In essence, cheap labor was not available in East Germany and was therefore not an incentive for private investments.

Since cheap labor was not available as an incentive for private investments, then other incentives would have been offered to entice private investments. The other main incentive a government can provide is tax incentives. Investment tax credits should have been generously offered and were not. But even if tax credits had been available, they would have been insufficient to *immediately* lure large-scale private investments into East Gemany. Therefore, the government should have started a crash program with infrastructure investments such as streets, office buildings, and environmental clean-up projects. Such government-sponsored investments would, at least in theory, have had the advantages that they could bypass bureaucratic hurdles easily and would have created a generally positive investment climate. Some—but not enough—government money was earmarked for early investments. It may be hard to believe, but even these government-sponsored initiatives got stuck in the bureaucratic maze. From the DM 3 billion ($1.9 billion) that the West German government had provided, only DM 100 million ($64 million) had made its way through the bureaucracy by September of 1990. Since neither generous tax incentives nor large government investments occurred, every economist could have predicted that the industrial production would plummet after the currency reform.

The West German government had the following model in mind when it started the transformation process. It believed that a small number of government-financed infrastructure investments and the expected retail boom would be sufficient to entice the private sector to invest heavily in East Germany. These investments were supposed to provide new jobs which would compensate for job losses from closings of noncompetitive corporations. In essence, the government hoped that a high level of economic activity would develop which would make the adjustments in specific industries easier and less frightening for the public.

The retail boom actually materialized, but it did not benefit the East German producers and retailers. The East Germans were tired of purchasing centrally planned goods and used their Deutsche Marks to buy Western goods which they considered to be state of the art. Thus, the strong spending by the East Germans did not revive their economy but instead turned West Germany's expansion into a boom. Also, the East German bureaucracy was hostile to the unfolding private initiative and the multitude of support requests by Western entrepreneurs and managers. Private investors faced an adverse investment climate. They were not welcomed with open arms and, worst of all, no competitive advantage promised an easy return for the invested money. Thus, private investments were not made in the magnitude the government had expected, and the number of new jobs did not compensate for the layoffs in obsolete industries.

By September at the latest, the West German officials should have known that their "development model" was not working and that East Germany would fall into a depression.[2] The term "depression" is a stark word, but it is more than justified because industrial production declined by 50 percent between December 1989 and December 1990.[3]

It is very interesting that Alexander Schalck–Golodkowski, the former East German secretary of state in the foreign trade ministry, revealed in an interview that in 1989 he and other high–ranking officials knew that East Germany was on the brink of economic disaster.[4] For years, East German officials had neglected the infrastructure of the country and had made almost no investments in the industrial and service sectors. They had used all the funds they could squeeze out of their economy and borrow from international lenders to pay for the overexpanded state apparatus. Schalck–Golodkowski went so far as to admit that he and others, politicians in the Soviet Union included, had known that the economic breakdown of East Germany was only a few years away. This statement, if correct, sheds new light on the Kremlin's willingness to give up East Germany. It is astonishing only that the degree of deterioration could escape the knowledge of Western governments and business partners. East Germany was an important producer of consumer staples for West Germany, and business contacts were well developed. For West German policy makers, these revelations should have been cause for alarm and immediate action.

What could be done under such circumstances? Economic theory recommends massive infrastructure investments and tax incentives for private investments. Infrastructure investments have the advantage of immediately creating jobs and upgrading the environment for private investments. Tax incentives are supposed to attract private investments because they improve their profitability.

Both measures are in the making. Kohl's cabinet is preparing a package consisting of large infrastructure investments and sizable tax incentives for private investments. DM 100 billion ($64.5 billion) will be available for public investments in 1991, and it is expected that this time the new East German state governments will make sure that the money is put to work immediately. Private investments will receive tax advantages amounting to 50 percent of the investment.[5] The postal ministry has given priority to the improvement of East German telephone service.[6] It is hard to imagine that one still cannot make a call from East to West Berlin. Three hundred thousand telephones and telephone lines will be installed in 1991. The transport ministry has just announced that it will start a highway improvement program of DM 2.5 billion ($1.6 billion) as soon as the winter weather breaks.[7] These are only a few examples of public investment programs that are ready to start at once.

Chancellor Kohl has realized, late but not too late, that the original model did not work and that massive infusions of capital and job opportunities are needed to turn the situation around.[8] His coalition partner, the F.D.P., and even the SPD were supporting these measures. But they were of such a magnitude that all layers of government and even the public were asked to participate in this solidarity program that was called "Community Work: Recovery East." It was difficult for Kohl to publicly admit that tax increases were needed after he had pledged that West Germans would not be asked for a financial contribution to the unification. But fiscal responsibility got the upper hand over political expediency. Kohl asked for a one–year income surtax of 7.5 percent. This and other tax measures were supposed to reduce the public deficit by one–third, or DM 46 billion ($29.7 billion) in 1991.[9]

But these measures will not prevent East Germany from falling more deeply into economic depression. At the end of February 1991, unemployment was 9 percent and people on short work reached 21 percent of the work force. Taking these numbers together, then 30 percent of the work force was either un– or underemployed. Heinrich Franke, president of the German unemployment compensation bureau, mentioned that by summer of 1991, half of the East German work force might be temporarily in this dismal situation.[10] The support decisions described above will be the key for a turnaround in the latter part of this year.

But the delay of a recovery in East Germany has already done significant damage to the social fabric in general and to the positive attitude toward free markets and competitive forces in particular. Some academics warn that this damage can be permanent if no turnaround occurs soon and that then it might take until a new generation has grown up before the social and economic gap between the two Germanies will completely disappear.

However, the present misery should not veil the long–term positive prospects of this unification. Volkswagen, Ford, Opel, Siemens, and Bosch—to name only some of the multinational concerns—have already begun to build huge new plants in East Germany. These plants will be state of the art and will be tough competition to older industrial sites in West Germany and elsewhere. These new plants will produce not only for the largest market in the world, the European Community, but might become the manufacturers for the East as well. East Germany's past could well be turned into an asset. Its familiarity with East Europeans and Russians could become the base for a growing trade with these countries. The problem seems "only" to be how to come from the depression–like situation of today to the recovery phase of tomorrow. For that, the "Community-Work: Recovery East" is a major step in the right direction. Chancellor Kohl's appeal to the East Germans said that it is now up to them to use the means and to turn the situation around. In 1990, the Treuhand has given 1,000 companies back into private hands, and another 300,000 East Germans have founded their own small companies. This demonstrates that private initiative is not dead and can be nurtured to success even after forty–five years of communist rule.

West Germany enjoyed an economic boom in 1990 mainly because East Germany's production and consumption went westward. The federal government's tax receipts rose an unexpected DM 35 billion ($22.6 billion), and the states gained DM 30 billion ($19.4 billion).[11] Now these additional tax receipts and more will flow back into East Germany. In a more general sense, West Germany can afford to pay for the reconstruction of East Germany. In the past five years, the West German population saved on the average approximately DM 390 billion ($252 billion), out of which about DM 120 billion ($77.4 billion) were not used for investments at home but exported.[12] Now a significant part of these capital exports will go to East Germany instead of other countries. Since investment opportunities in countries with stable political institutions are rare, East Germany will become an opportunity and will lose its character of being a burden in a matter of years. A large part of the funds flowing to East Germany should not be considered as the cost of unification but as the down payment on a profitable future in the larger united Germany. Germany is rejuvenated; it has gotten a new, inspiring task in its economic and business life. German entrepreneurs and managers will find ample opportunities at their doorstep and do not need to go into developing countries with all of their additional political risks. The prediction is easy to make that in a few years from now, the present woes will have given way to a steady and long-term recovery from which all Germans will benefit.

CONCLUSION

ONE FINAL LOOK BACK AND A FEW REMARKS ABOUT THE FUTURE

In the preceding essay, a great deal of evidence was presented to show that the German unification occurred in 1990 because three factors came together in a most fortunate way. The first factor was that the Soviet communist system brought a man to the top who wanted to invigorate the ailing communist system. Gorbachev knew that he had to do two things if he wanted to be successful: to free resources in the international and military arena and devote them to domestic needs, and to change the international political environment in such a way that Western know–how and financial means would be available for the reconstruction of the communist economy. In short, Gorbachev needed to end the sharp division between the East and West and to overcome the superpower competition. He offered, and the U. S. accepted, a change in the superpower relations which in turn reduced the importance of the iron curtain in Europe. It took from 1985 to 1989 until the developments, particularly in the East but also in the West, created an opportunity to overcome the division in Europe. The Soviet Union was prepared to give up its dominance over Eastern Europe. This gave Germany the chance to overcome its division and unity, although not many people realized as much in 1989. In essence, Gorbachev's reform movement gave Europe the unique opportunity to overcome the consequences of World War II and to grow together again.

But the East German leadership opposed reforms, correctly fearing that reforms could lead to the demise of the communist system and subsequently of their own rule and privileged status. The impetus for change in East Germany had to come from somewhere else. The East German people, like the people of other East European states, had the courage to become the driving force first for reforms and later for the destruction of their state and the unification with

West Germany. The East Germans took their fate into their own hands and succeeded in unseating a government which had all the instruments of power at its disposal. Perhaps the most remarkable feature of this revolution was that it occurred in such a disciplined way.

Discipline and nonviolence removed the communist regime's option to use brute force. State brutality against non-violent demonstrators in front of Western TV cameras would have discredited the Honecker regime and Gorbachev's image as a reformer. Thus, Honecker did not dare to use his security apparatus. But without the use of the full power of the state, the communist regime could not quell public protest and survive.

The people in East Germany were able to destroy the communist system, but they would not have been able to achieve the unification with West Germany on their own. The unification of East and West Germany was imbedded in many other larger international political problems. These problems needed attention before a unification became feasible. A respected member of the international community had to take up the people's demand for unification and had to integrate this demand into the larger international issues that had to be addressed first. Chancellor Kohl of West Germany realized earlier than others that the chance was real for doing what all West German politicians had wanted to do since the end of World War II: to bring about the unification of Germany in peaceful negotiations.[1] Kohl and his Foreign Minister Genscher were modest enough to know that they needed the U. S., the strongest of the victorious Allies, as their advocate to overcome the resistance of the other Allies, the Soviet Union in particular. In the ensuing negotiations, the relations between the superpowers, the situation in Europe, and finally the size and role of Germany were expected to change. Thus, Germany could be the initiator and the driving force behind the negotiations, but it needed the support of the U. S. for a successful conclusion.

The presence and interplay of these three factors—the change in the international situation, the people's revolution in East Germany, and the presence of an astute, well-connected negotiator on Germany's behalf—were all necessary conditions for the successful realignment of global politics and the unification of Germany. If any one of those factors had not been in place in 1989 and 1990, then the unification might not have happened or it might have been achieved in quite a different way. If, for example, West Germany had been governed by the Social–Democrat Oskar Lafontaine, the outcome would have been quite different.

The window of opportunity for such significant changes in global, European, and German politics was open only for a limited period of time. As the ratification process for unification and related treaties in Moscow's parliament demonstrated, the forces of restoration demanded additional concessions and recognized, but did not ratify, the terms of the troop withdrawal from East Germany.[2]

Fritz Ullrich Fack, a senior correspondent of the *Frankfurter Allgemeine Zeitung* wrote that:

> The Germans in East and West are united in their opinion that in global politics, the door to unification was opened a little bit for a historic second of time in 1990. It was neither wrong nor hasty to grab this unique chance; today, we know that this chance would not have been offered again.[3]

Many German politicians share the conviction that today, unification would either not be possible or would occur only under very different conditions.

The Germans tried to keep a low profile and to prevent exuberance during the celebration on October 3, 1990, and thereafter. It is a good omen that Germany has learned its historic lesson and realizes that it is in the center of Europe, not only the bridge between East and West but also the place where statemanship is needed to keep a balance between all the forces and demands that have so often torn Europe apart. Helmut Schmidt, for example, warned that:

> Nobody should believe that the Germans can do what they please beginning October, 3. The contrary is true: not only our economic but also our foreign and European political tasks will be more difficult than they have been in decades. . . . The Polish and the French nations will continue to be our most important neighbors.[4]

Those warning words cannot veil that a fundamental change has occurred in the center of Europe. The frontier between East and West moved eastward; how far eastward, only the future will tell.

Germany, now the largest and economically strongest country in Europe, is no longer the border state to the East but at the center of an emerging Europe that could include the East European states and perhaps even the Soviet Union. Today, Germans and their politicians hesitate to take over the political responsibility that comes with economic leadership. But over time, this hesitation, caused by two world wars, will abate. However, politicians who hope that Germany will simply take some responsibility from other shoulders will be disappointed. Theo Sommer, the influential editor of *Die Zeit*, summarized people's opinions by saying that Germans will resist becoming again a player of power politics.[5] They are foremost concerned about humanitarian and environmental problems and they want their country to play only a minor role—similar to the one of Switzerland—in international politics. German governments will have to take those well articulated and strongly supported demands into account if they want to remain in office for any length of time.

But Germany's economic weight will eventually force greater responsibilities on Germany. Before such responsibilities can be accepted by the public, all aspects of the unification have to be positively resolved. Germany gained political unification on October 3, 1990. Since then, it has become obvious that much goodwill from both sides and great economic efforts will be needed to also bring about a social and human unification. Chancellor Kohl has admitted that he underestimated the degree of devastation in both economic resources and private initiative which the communist system left behind; thus, he pleaded with the Germans in East and West not to increase the cleavage between them but to develop empathy and cooperate with each other.[6] As soon as Kohl and his cabinet realized the depth of the problem, they not only made money available but also promised personal efforts to improve relations between the two parts of the country. Chancellor Kohl will frequently visit East Germany until the river Elbe has ceased to be a border between two Germanies. He argued that it will take between three and five years before the social and human cleavage will have totally disappeared. Some political analysts are more skeptical; they fear that a new generation must grow up in the free–market environment before the invisible border between the Germans will disappear.[7] The April 1, 1991, murder of Detlev Karsten Rohwedder, chairman of the Treuhandgesellschaft (Trust Company), responsible for the reprivatization of East Germany's industry, indicated how tense the atmosphere has become.[8]

The transition from a planned to a free–market economy in East Germany cannot be used as an example for other East European states. East Germany was in the unique position of having a wealthy democratic other half, which was both a blessing and source of additional difficulties. The blessing was that East Germany was forced to give up totally its communist past and to take over a proven democratic free–market system that had one of the strongest social welfare components of any capitalistic system. The source of additional difficulties was that a rich and a poor part will be required to live side by side until the initiative of the East and the generosity of the West have leveled the differences.

A similar situation does not exist anywhere in Eastern Europe. There the people have no "safe haven." They must develop the political and economic infrastructures themselves, and they must suffer alone through the difficult transition from communist tutelage to independent government. In all of these countries, a strong, ethnically based nationalism is on the rise. All of them lack democratic experience and are saddled with obsolete industries. These countries have large foreign debts and great difficulties attracting aid or foreign investments. All of them are going through deep economic troubles that exacerbate the problems of transition.[9] Therefore, it is difficult to predict what kind of government and economic order will emerge. However, it is in the very interests of Western Europe that at least Poland, Czechoslovakia, and Hungary are managing a successful transition. They will be the new border or buffer states between the democratic West and the Soviet Union. And there can be no question that the development in Europe will be overshadowed by the events in the Soviet Union.

REFERENCES

PART I.

The Political Situation in Spring of 1989

1. Stephen Larrabee wrote, "It has been Gorbachev's campaign for greater *glasnost* (openness) and democratization, however, that has made some East European leaderships the most uncomfortable." F. Stephen Larrabee, "Eastern Europe: A Generational Change," *Foreign Policy*, No. 70, Spring 1988, p. 49.

2. Charles Gati wrote, "While East Germany shows its fear of *glasnost*, Hungary is racing ahead of Gorbachev." Charles Gati, "Eastern Europe On Its Own," *Foreign Affairs*, Vol. 68, No. 1, 1988/89, p. 109.

3. Tad Szulc, "Poland's Path," *Foreign Policy*, No. 72, Fall 1988, pp. 210–229.

4. Corneliu Bogdan argued, "Eastern Europe today . . . is the region undergoing the fastest social change on the continent." "Crossing The European Divide," *Foreign Policy*, No. 75, Summer 1989, p. 56.

5. Also Hamilton argued in fall of 1989, "The GDR is not ripe for a revolution, but it has entered an important phase of transition." Daniel Hamilton, "The Wall Behind the Wall," *Foreign Policy*, No. 76, Fall 1989, p. 195.

6. Valery Giscard d'Estaing, Yasuhiro Nakasone, and Henry A. Kissinger, "East–West Relations," *Foreign Affairs*, Vol. 68, No. 3, Summer 1989, pp. 1–21.

7. These are some of the most influential publications about the decline of communism:

Zbigniew Brzezinski, *The Grand Failure* (New York: Charles Scribner's Sons, 1989).

Zbigniew Brzezinski, "Post–Communist Nationalism," *Foreign Affairs*, Vol. 68, No. 5, pp. 1–25.

Mikhail Gorbachev, *Perestroika* (New York: Harper & Row, 1987).

8. The thesis of the decline of U. S. dominance in the world received wide publicity. Paul Kennedy's account is perhaps the most influential publication about this subject. As one could have expected, his arguments were countered by distinguished scholars. Joseph S. Nye, Jr., and Henry R. Nau's essays are the most comprehensive rebuttles.

Paul Kennedy, *The Rise and Fall of The Great Powers* (New York: Random House, 1987).

Joseph S. Nye, *Bound to Lead* (New York: Basic Books, 1990).

Henry R. Nau, *The Myth Of America's Decline* (New York: Oxford University Press, 1990).

Part II

A. The Reform Movement in September and October of 1989

1. On September 10, 1990, in an interview with Hannes Burger, correspondent of *Die Welt*, Gyula Horn, the former foreign minister of Hungary, gave a detailed account of the opening of the Hungarian border. "Wichtig war nur, an der Seite der Deutschen zu stehen," *Das Jahr der Deutschen Einheit*, ed. Die Welt (Berlin: Ullstein Verlag, 1990), pp. 36–39.

2. *The Economist* reported, "On a cool evening last Sunday, thousands of East Germans crossed the border from Hungary to Austria. . . . Less than 72 hours later, some 12,000 East Germans had found their way up into West Germany. *The Economist*, September 16, 1989, pp. 49–50.

In the eighties, East Germany's communists found some sympathy among left–leaning SPD politicians. For example, Hans Eppler, party leader in Baden–Wuerttemberg, was convinced that the division of the world into East and West would not change in the foreseeable future. Therefore, he wanted to reduce the tensions at the border between the two blocs, and in particular between the two Germanies. He argued that a second German state with its own citizenship would be a much more self–assured political entity and would make humanitarian concessions easier than it would feel free to do without an assurance of its independence. He also believed that over a period of time both systems, the capitalistic and the socialistic ones, would and should move toward each other to make a unification eventually possible. The East Germans were fortunate that Eppler never came to power. They had their German passports and were able to move legally to the West.

SPD, "Das gemeinsame Papier der Grundweertekommission der SPD und der Akademie fuer Gesellschaftswissenschaften der SED," *Frankfurter Allgemeine Zeitung*, August 28, 1987.

Gesine Schwan, "Eine Januskopf Gefahren und Chancen," *Frankfurter Allgemeine Zeitung*, September 23, 1987.

Erhard Eppler, *Wie Feuer und Wasser, Sind Ost und West friedensfaehig* (Hamburg: Rowohlt Verlag, 1988).

The Economist wrote, "Social Democrats did indeed believe they could encourage reform in East Germany 'from the top down,' that is, by influencing Mr. Honecker and his pals." "Germanies in Confusion," *The Economist*, October 7, 1989, pp. 55–56.

4. Detlev Ahlers, "Bevor die Zuege rollten: Die dramatischen Stunden in Prag," ed. Die Welt, *Das Jahr Der Deutschen Einheit*, (Berlin: Ullstein Verlag, 1990), pp. 51–54.

5. *The Economist*, "Waiting for Gorbachev," *The Economist*, September 30, 1989.

6. On October 1, 1989, 6,000 East Germans were transported on special trains fram Prague to West Germany. On October 4, another train with 10,000 people followed. Schwartau/Steinberg, *Berlin im November* (Berlin: Nicolaische Verlagsbuchhandlung, 1990), p. 147.

7. The first prominent article about the vague possibility of a unification of Germany was published by *The Economist*. There it was reiterated, "Given the choice, therefore, the rest of the West would prefer the Germanies to remain separate, communing freely with each other as Bavarians commune with Austrians, with no barbed wire in sight." *The Economist*, June 17, 1989, pp. 13–14.

Theo Sommer wrote, "The stream of refugees moves the nation. The people demand an assertive reunification policy. But there is no way; the German question is not on the agenda right now!" Theo Sommer, "Kleine Schritte oder grosse Luftspruenge," *Die Zeit*, No. 39, September 29, 1989.

8. Werner Harenberg, "Sindermann ueber Macht und Ende der SED," *Der Spiegel*, May 7, 1990, pp. 19–53.

9. Helmut Schmidt, "Ein Aufstand gegen Zwang und Luege," *Die Zeit*, No. 46., November 17, 1989.

Helmut Kohl, "Selbstbestimmung ist and bleibt das Herzstueck unserer Deutschlandspolitik, *Frankfurter Allgemeine Zeitung*, November 9, 1989.

10. On November 4, a group named "Artists for Democracy" called for a mass demonstration. One million people participated in East Berlin. That brought the Honecker regime down. Schwartau/Steinberg, *Berlin im November*, (Berlin: Nicolaische Verlagsbuchhandlung, 1990), p. 149.

11. "Enter a New Anti–Hero," *The Economist*, November 21, 1989, pp. 49–50.

"Hurtling into the Unknown," *The Economist*, November 11, 1989, pp. 55–56.

B. The Revolution in Winter 1989/1990

1. "When the party's over," *The Economist*, November 18, 1989, pp. 51–53.

2. Die Welt, ed., *Das Jahr Der Deutschen Einheit* (Berlin: Ullstein Verlag, 1990), p. 309.

3. In an interview with the *Chicago Tribune* right in time for the first anniverary of the fall of the Berlin Wall, Egon Krenz tried to give the impression that the opening of the Wall on November 9, 1989, was more an accident than a calculated political move. However, many Western observers are not convinced that the border police would have opened the Wall without clear instructions from the top. If Krenz's account is correct after all, then the communist leadership was in much deeper disarray at that time than has been assummed so far. Reprint of the interview "Fall of Berlin Wall Was More a Comedy of Errors Than by Design," *San Diego Union*, November 4, 1990.

4. On the weekend following the opening of the Berlin Wall on November 9, 1989, three million East Germans flooded into West Berlin, received DM 100 as welcoming money, and and were welcomed with open arms by millions of West Berliners. In the weeks following November 9, another three to five million East Germans crossed the

border into West Germany after waiting in their little Trabants at the checkpoints for as much as ten hours. The East German authorities felt obligated to open new border crossings almost daily. On December 24, East Germany finally dropped the demand that East Germans needed a passport and visa before leaving East Germany. Then all controls vanished and the waiting time at the border crossings normalized.

Dieter Rose und Hanns–Ruediger Karutz, "Man moechte alle, die kommen, in die Arme nehmen," *Das Jahr Der Deutschen Einheit,* ed. Die Welt (Berlin: Ullstein Verlag, 1990) pp. 74–80.

5. Wolfgang Gessler, "Beim Parteimarathon blieb die Frage nach dem Sieger offen," Rose and Karutz, pp. 100–103.

6. Dieter Dose and Hans–Ruediger Karutz, "Die Opposition speist sich aus vielen Quellen," Rose and Karutz, pp. 42–45.

7. Werner Maser, *Helmut Kohl, Der Deutsche Kanzler* (Berlin: Ullstein Verlag, 1990), pp. 310–311.

8. Nina Grunenberg, "Blick in die Geschichte, Vor einem Jahr wurde Hans Modrow abgewaehlt," *Die Zeit,* No. 12, March 22, 1991.

9. Werner Maser, *Helmut Kohl, Der Deutsche Kanzler* (Berlin: Ullstein Verlag, 1990), pp. 314–315.

10. In November and December of 1989, the leading German politicians still talked about closer cooperation between the two independent German states. Chancellor Kohl had presented his "tenpoint program" of unification in the Bundestag on November 28. There he argued that the question of East and West Germany belonging to two opposing security pacts must be resolved before unification could take place. However, in his private meeting with Gorbachev on February 10, Chancellor Kohl found that both could be accomplished in 1990—the resolution of the European security question and the unification of Germany. The SPD continued to favor the existence of two German states for a longer period of time. Oskar Lafontaine, in particular, wanted to postpone the unification until after Europe had grown together. Hans Modrow, minister president of East Germany, argued for a contractual agreement (*Vertragsgemeinschaft*) between two independent German states. "Word Games," *The Economist,* December 23, 1989, p. 58.

11. Elisabeth Noelle–Neumann, "Nationalgefuehl Als Historisches Ereignis," Documentation by the Allensbach Institute for the article in the *Frankfurter Allgemeine Zeitung,* February 22, 1990.

12. Werner Maser, *Helmut Kohl, Der Deutsche Kanzler* (Berlin: Ullstein Verlag, 1990), pp. 308–312.

13. Werner Maser, *Helmut Kohl*, p. 319.

14. Chancellor Kohl said in an interview with *Die Bild Zeitung*: "The elections in the GDR are in ten days. Then Modrow's tenure is a thing of the past. I find what Modrow has to say now to be insignificant. . . . Modrow is a candidate of the successor organization to the communist party. And when I listen to his party friend, Gysi, then I realize that these people have learned nothing. They are responsible for the bankruptcy of the GDR. But now they act as if they had nothing to do with the past." *The Bild Zeitung*, March 8, 1990.

Nina Grunenberg, "Der richtige Riecher, Helmut Kohl, Kanzler der Einheit," *Die Zeit*, No. 40, October 5, 1990.

15. The following arguments were often advanced that the events in East Germany do not qualify as a genuine revolution.

A. The communist regime was brought down by the withdrawal of the protection by the Red Army and not by the East German people.

B. Revolutions physically eliminate a ruling class and replace it with a new one.

C. The East Germans seemed to be preoccupied with the desire for more and better consumer goods and only secondarily interested in political change.

Robert Darnton rejected these and other arguments and suggested that modern revolutions accomplish their goal of installing a new political elite without physically destroying the old one. Robert Darnton, "Did East Germany Have a Revolution," *New York Times*, December 3, 1990.

C. The Election of March 18, 1990

1. Professor Elisabeth Noelle–Neumann wrote, based on opinion research, that, ". . . the East German population is ill prepared for the discussion of fundamental political questions. The meaning of freedam for a government system is emotionally appreciated, but the connection between freedom and a free market system is not understood by a large part of the population. Many believe that the

implementation of a free market system is also possible under socialist rule. A systemic contradiction between socialism and freedom is not accepted by the young generation. Elisabeth Noelle–Neumann, "Diffuse Meinungen zu Diktatur und Demokratie," *Frankfurter Allgemeine Zeitung*, February 22, 1990.

2. "Vierundzwanzig Parteien bewerben sich um die Stimmem in der DDR," *Frankfurter Allgemeine Zeitung*, March 12, 1990.

3. Fritz Richter, "Die SPD war ein Teil der SED geworden," *Frankfurter Allgemeine Zeitung*, December 28, 1990.

4. Serge Schmemann, "Bonn's Politicans Invade East Germany," *New York Times*, February 9, 1990.

5. Elisabeth Noelle–Neumann, "Ein demokratischer Wahlkampf gab den Ausschlag,", *Die Zeit*, March 23, 1990.

6. "Lafontaine in Leipzig: Waehrungsunion nicht zu schnell, Massnahmen gegen den Uebersiedlerstrom gefordert," *Frankfurter Allgemeine Zeitung*, February 24, 1990.

Eckehard Fuhr, "Der dissonante Doppelklang von Ibrahim und Oskar," *Frankfurter Allgemeine Zeitung*, February 26, 1990.

7. Wolfgang Jaeger, "Der alte Kanzlerwahlverein ist tot," *Frankfurter Allgemeine Zeitung*, March 1, 1990.

8. "Liberale Parteien treten als 'Bund Freier Demokraten' zur Wahl an. Zusammenschluss von LDP, Ost–FDP und Deutscher Forumspartei," *Frankfurter Allgemeine Zeitung*, February 13, 1990.

9. Werner Maser, *Helmut Kohl, Der Deutsche Kanzler* (Berlin: Ullstein Verlag, 1990), pp, 319–330.

10. Elisabeth Noelle–Neumann, "Ein demokratischer Wahlkampf gab den Ausschlag," *Die Zeit*, March 23, 1990.

11. Ibid.

12. "In der neuen Volkskammer Abgeordnete aus 12 Parteien," *Frankfurter Allgemeine Zeitung*, March 23, 1990.

Peter Jochen Winters, "Schwarz und Rot verteilen sich: Nord und Sued wie in der Bundesrepublik," *Frankfurter Allgemeine Zeitung*, March 20, 1990.

13. Helmut Schmidt, "Schritt um Schritt zur Einheit," *Die Zeit*, No. 13, March 30, 1990.

14. Christian Wernicke, "Nach schwierigen Verhandlungen stellt Lothar de Maiziere sein Koalitions-Kabinett vor," *Die Zeit*, No. 16, April 20, 1990.

15. On May 6, 1990, the first local democratic elections were

held in East Germany. The outcome confirmed the leading role of
the conservative parties:

Results of the Local Elections in East Germany
May 6, 1990

	May Result	For Comparison March 18
CDU	34.4	40.9
SPD	21.3	21.8
PDS	14.6	16.3
F.D.P.	6.7	5.3
DSU	3.4	6.3
Other Parties	19.6	9.4

At the local level, many small groups and parties gained votes,
particularly at the expense of the CDU. "Die Parteien zufrieden
mit dem Ergebnis der DDR–Kommualwahlen," *Frankfurter Allgemeine Zeitung*, June 8, 1990.

PART III

A. The Problems Surrounding The Unification

1. Oskar Lafontaine, *Deutsche Wahrheiten* (Hamburg: Hoffmann
& Campe Verlag, 1990).

David Gress, "The Politics of German Unification," ed. Nils H.
Wessell, *The New Europe: Revolution in East-West Relations*
(New York: The Academy of Political Science, 1991).

2. Peter Glotz, *Der Irrweg des Nationalstaates* (Stuttgart: Deutsche
Verlags–Anstalt, 1990).

3. Werner Maser, *Helmut Kohl, der Deutsche Kanzler* (Berlin:
Ullstein Verlag, 1990), pp. 297–330.

4. Until spring of 1990, the Soviet Union categorily denied that
a "German question" existed at all. They argued that the reform
movement would transform the communist into a socialistic state
that would have a bright future inside the Soviet hemisphere. Jens
Hacker, "Lange wurde in Moskau die Existenz einer deutschen Frage
geleugnet," *Frankfurter Allgemeine Zeitung*, May 28, 1990.

5. Claus Genrich, "Moskau will die deutsche Einheit bald bei vorerst eingeschraenkter Souveraenitaet, Innere und aeussere Aspekte entkoppeln," *Frankfurter Allgemeine Zeitung*, May 7, 1990.

6. "Germany sets syllabus for the new maths of Europe," *The Economist*, May 5, 1990.

7. Christoph Bertram provides an excellent overview of the problems caused by the German unification for Europe, the superpower relations, and the international order, in Christoph Bertram, "The German Question," *Foreign Affairs*, Vol. 69, No. 2, Spring 1990, pp. 45–62.

B. The Settlement of the International Questions Surrounding the Unification

1. Jeanne J. Kirkpatrick argued, "The postwar era collapsed in 1989. . . . The division of Europe had been overcome symbolically with the collapse of the Berlin Wall, and literally with the progressive opening of borders between Hungary and Austria, Czechoslovakia and Austria, and East Germany and West Germany." "Beyond the Cold War," *Foreign Affairs*, Vol. 69, No. 1, 1989/90, p. 1.

2. Arnold L. Horelick argued, "At the Malta summit between Presidents George Bush and Mikhail Gorbachev, the convergence of American and Soviet positions on most agenda items was unprecedented. Their relationship seemed likely to develop with minimum tension, low risk, and, prospectively, at greatly reduced costs." "U. S.–Soviet Relations: Threshold of a New Era," *Foreign Affairs*, Vol. 69, No. 1, 1989/90, p. 51.

3. Sheila Rule, "A British Official, Stirring Outcry, Says Germans Are Taking Over," *New York Times*, July 13, 1990.

4. *Time*, March 26, 1990, p. 36.

5. Helmut Kohl, "Europe—Every German's Future," *European Affairs*, No. 1, Spring 1990, pp. 16–21.

6. Ronald D. Asmus wrote, "Washington's early and forthright support for the German unification was well received and has helped to consolidate America's stature in West Germany." "A United Germany," *Foreign Affairs*, Vol. 69, No. 2, Spring 1990, p. 72.

7. Friedman and Gordon gave a detailed account about the emergence of the two–plus–four negotiations at the NATO conference in Ottawa. Thomas L. Friedman and Michael R. Gordon, "Steps to

German Unity: Bonn as a Power," *New York Times*, February 16, 1990.

8. Christoph Bertram, "Eine Geduldsprobe fuer die Deutschen," *Die Zeit*, No. 20, May 18, 1990.

9. Anne–Marie Burley examines the reasons why Germany should not be united at this point in time, in "The Once and Future German Question," *Foreign Affairs*, Vol. 68, No. 5, Winter 1989/90, pp. 65–83.

10. The economic and political stability of East Germany crumbled in the summer months of 1990. On June 17, during the celebration of the people's uprising in East Berlin in 1953, the East German party DSU spontaneously requested the immediate "Anschluss" (merger) of East Germany with West Germany in the parliamentary session. Two–thirds of the house voted for the adoption of this resolution. Only the tactical maneuvering of Minister–President de Maiziere and the opposition of the present Chancellor Kohl prevented a final adoption of this resolution. *Frankfurter Allgemeine Zeitung*, June 18, 1990.

11. Craig R. Whitney, "Promise of Yalta: Redeemed at Last?," *New York Times*, July 17, 1990.

12. Manfred Woerner, "NATO's New Decade," *European Affairs*, No. 1, Spring 1990, pp. 8–15.

13. Gerald Seib, "NATO Agrees to Alter Defense Strategy in Aftermath of Communism's Collapse," *New York Times*, July 6, 1990.

14. Serge Schmemann, "Gorbachev Clears the Way for Unification of Germany," *New York Times*, July 17, 1990.

15. "Nach den Verabredungen von Paris ist ein Friedensvertrag nicht mehr noetig," *Frankfurter Allgemeine Zeitung*, July 19, 1990.

16. Robert Leicht, "Den Frieden mit Deutschland gemacht," *Die Zeit*, No. 30, July 27, 1990.

Serge Schemann, "And the Past is Quietly Buried," *New York Times*, September 13, 1990.

Thomas L. Friedman, "Four Allies Give Up Rights in Germany," *New York Times*, September 13, 1990.

"Vertrag ueber gute Nachbarschaft, Partnerschaft und Zusammenarbeit, *Frankfurter Allgemeine Zeitung*, September 14, 1990.

17. Over and above the DM 12 billion for moving the Red Army back into the Soviet Union, West Germany contributed to the stationing costs of the Red Army in East Germany. West Germany paid

DM 1.5 billlion ($970,000) in May of 1990 and agreed to provide an interest-free loan of DM 3 billion ($1.94 billion) to cover the future expenses. Peter Neckermann, "Germans Hope Gigantic Price is Historic Value," *The Columbus Dispatch*, September 30, 1990.

18. The dispute with Poland over the German–Polish border was settled at the two–plus–four meeting in Paris. There Germany agreed to sign a treaty with Poland recognizing the present border as final soon after the unification on October 3, 1990. Germany also forgave a loan of DM 750,000. Walter S. Mossberg, "German Unification Cleared As Pact with Poland Is Set," *Wall Street Journal*, July 18, 1990.

C. The Economic, Social, And Monetary Union

1. Ferdinand Protzman, "Vital Merger Step, Political Pressure Seen Outweighing the Risk of a Rise in Inflation," *New York Times*, April 24, 1990.

Ferdinand Protzman, "German Leaders Agree on a July 2 Unification Date," *New York Times*, April 25, 1990.

2. East Germany's productivity was established to be about 30 to 35 percent of that of West Germany, and the argument was that the wages had to reflect this if East Germany wanted to be competitive with the West. "Bonner Streit um den Umstellungskurs bei Loehnen und Renten," *Frankfurter Allgemeine Zeitung*, March 30, 1990.

3. Otto Schlecht, secretary of state in the ministry of economics, argued that the German model of a free–market system is best suited for implementation by East Germany and other East Bloc countries who want to leave the communist system of state planning behind. "Ein Modell macht Karriere," *Frankfurter Allgemeine Zeitung*, March 3, 1990.

4. The Institut der Deutschen Wirtschaft of Cologne argued that East Germany can best be compared with Taiwan or Korea. If a free–market system would be introduced, then it would take off like the economic development in these two countries did about a decade ago. "Marktwirtschaftliche Reformen sind der Schluessel zum Erfolg," *Frankfurter Allgemeine Zeitung*, March 27, 1990.

5. Chancellor Kohl made public that the small savers would receive an exchange rate of 1 : 1 for their saving accounts. This

announcement came on March 13, five days before the election. Ferdinand Protzmann, "Bonn Sets Mark Rate On Savings," *New York Times*, March 14, 1990.

6. The stream of immigrants from East to West Germany was a serious concern for both governments. Tens of thousands of East Germans tried to find work and shelter in West Germany: 74,000 in January, 64,000 in February, 64,000, and 46,000 in March. "Bonner Mahnung an alle Deutschen, Die Einheit erfordert Kraft und Mut," *Frankfurter Allgemeine Zeitung*, April 28, 1990.

7. The first state treaty or unification treaty about the economic, social, and monetetary union was signed in Bonn on May 18, 1990. De Maiziere told the press that fellow Germans had negotiated in good faith and had reached a fair compromise. He said, "This is the first step toward unification." "Ein bedeutsamer Schritt zur Einheit," *Frankfurter Allgemeine Zeitung*, May 19, 1990.

8. Terence Roth, "Bonn, States Agree to Form Big Unity Fund, Debt Will be Used to Create $74.2 Billion Facility to Aid East Germany," *New York Times*, May 16, 1990.

9. The exchange from East Mark into DM occurred on favorable terms for the East Germans:

A. Wages, rents, leases, and other income payments were exchanged at the rate of 1 : 1.

B. The social security system was integrated into West Germany's system. This meant that future social security payments in DM were as high as or higher than they were in East German Marks before.

C. Private savings were exchanged in the following way:

(1) People sixty years and older could exchange up to 6,000 East Marks at the rate of 1 : 1.

(2) People between 15 and 59 could exchange up to 4,000 East Marks at the rate of 1 : 1.

(3) People under the age of 15 could exchange up to 2,000 East Marks at the rate of 1 : 1.

(4) All other savings were exchanged at the rate of 2 : 1.

D. Foreigners or foreign institutions that possessed East German Marks could exchange those at the rate of 3 : 1.

E. All private and coporate debt was devalued at a rate of 2 : 1.

10. "Aus 447 Milliarden DDR–Mark wurden 246 Milliarden DM–Mark," *Frankfurter Allgemeine Zeitung,* July 23, 1990.

11. In this very short period of time, the Deutsche Bundesbank in cooperation with the banking business provided 10,000 places where money could be exchanged on July 2. Each person was entitled to receive DM 2,000 in cash if he so wanted. "Am 1. Juli zahlen 10,000 Stellen D–Mark aus," *Frankfurter Allgemeine Zeitung,* May 28, 1990.

D. The Economic Recovery That Did Not Materialize

1. The people have forgotten that the introduction of the DM in 1949 was only the beginning of a long road to better living conditions. It took years before unemployment had subsided and most West Germans again enjoyed decent living conditions. The sometimes slow recovery turned into a boom only when the Korean War changed the global economic situation. "The New Germany, D–mark day dawns," *The Economist,* June 30, 1990. Survey pp. 1–22.

2. The West German economic system is often imprecisely called a capitalistic system. Ludwig Erhard, the father of the German economic miracle, called the West German system a "social–free–market system," a term selected to indicate Erhard's and the ruling Christian Democrat's deep commitment toward social justice and the protection of the underpriviledged. Erhard made it unmistakably clear that West Germany wanted to introduce an economic system in which market forces ruled and a strong welfare component would take care of the people in need. Germany's system combined the instruments of competition and solidarity in a unique way. Professor Kurt H. Biedenkopf wrote, "In the history of mankind it is a rare event that dream s of generations finally become reality. It was Ludwig Erhard who has realized the dreams that mankind had since the industrial revolution began in the nineteenth century for a free, social, just, and responsive economic and social system." Karl Hohmann, ed., *Ludwig Erhard Erbe und Auftrag,* (Duesseldorf–Wien: Econ Verlag, 1977), p. 77.

3. Theo Sommer, "An der Schwelle zur deutschen Einheit: Rueckblick und Ausblick," *Die Zeit,* No. 27, July 6, 1990.

Karl Schiller, "Freikarten werden nicht verteilt," *Frankfurter Allgemeine Zeitung,* June 30, 1990.

4. "Wenn die Treuhandanstalt zur Inflationsmaschine wird," *Frankfurter Allgemeine Zeitung*, July 3, 1990.

5. Peter Christ, "Wunder dauern etwas laenger," *Die Zeit*, No. 46, November 16, 1990.

6. Marie–Luise Hauch–Fleck, "Endspurt der Eigentuemer," *Die Zeit*, No. 43, October 26, 1990.

7. "Treuhand will bis Januar 500 Betriebe verkaufen," *Frankfurter Allgemeine Zeitung*, October 27, 1990.

8. By mid–October the following number of civil servants commuted daily from Cologne (Bonn's airport) to East Germany:

Bonn's Civil Servants Commuting to East Germany

Ministry of Foreign Affairs	10 persons
Ministry of Foreign Aid	8 persons
Ministry of the Interior	30 persons
Ministry of Finance	45 persons
Ministry of Economics	40 persons
Ministry of Agriculture	21 persons
Ministry of Labor	6 persons
Ministry of Defense	50 persons
Ministry of Health	25 persons
Ministry of Transport	40 persons
Ministry of Environment	12 persons
Ministry of Postal Service	3 persons
Ministry of Construction	5 persons
Ministry of Research	12 persons
	307 persons

"Der Beamtenshuttle fliegt arbeitstaeglich nach Berlin," *Frankfurter Allgemeine Zeitung*, October 18, 1990.

9. "Die Lohnpolitik in der DDR ein schwieriger Balanceakt," *Frankfurter Allgemeine Zeitung*, June 28, 1990.

10. Roger de Weck, "Was noch zum Wohlstand fehlt," *Die Zeit*, No. 28, July 13, 1990.

Peter Christ, "Rosskur ohne Medizin," *Die Zeit*, No. 33, August 17, 1990.

Helmut Schmidt, "Das grosse Glueck der Freiheit," *Die Zeit*, No. 34, August 24, 1990.

11. Interview with Klaus–Peter Kantzer, member of the managing Board (Vorstand) of Schering AG., Berlin, on December 22, 1990, in Berlin.

12. Interview with Professor Carl Hahn, Chairman and CEO of Volkswagen AG., Wolfsburg, in Kronberg, October 7, 1990.

13. "A Snapshot of West German Goods Sold in East Germany," *Die Zeit*, No. 39, September 29, 1990.

14. "Vierundachtzig Prozent kauften ein Gebrauchtauto," *Frankfurter Allgemeine Zeitung*, November 19, 1990.

15. "Jetzt fast 1.8 Millionen Kurzarbeiter im Osten," *Frankfurter Allgemeine Zeitung*, January 9, 1991.

16. Heinrich Franke, president of the unemployment compensation bureau, reported that at the end of 1990, 642,200 East Germans or 7.3 percent of the 8.9 million work force were unemployed. Another 1.8 million people were on short work, meaning that they got about 90 percent of their net income for partial or no work. He argued that the trough at the unemployment situation was not yet reached and that about DM 20 billion ($12.9 billion) would be needed for unemployment compensation in 1991. In West Germany, the number of jobs increased by a record of 750,000 to 28.8 million in 1990. Unemployment declined to 6.4 percent, down from 7.1 percent at the end of December 1989. *Frankfurter Allgemeine Zeitung*, January 9, 1991.

17. "Im Westen das kraeftigste Wachstum seit 1976," *Frankfurter Allgemeine Zeitung*, January 11, 1991.

18. "Seit Juli kommen 100,000 Personen in den Westen," *Frankfurter Allgemeine Zeitung*, November 23, 1990.

The German Interior Ministry reported that the following number of people came from East to West Germany (numbers are approximate):

May 1989 to October 1989	45,700 people
October 1989 to December 1989	233,674 people
January 1990 to June 1990	238,384 people
July 1990 to February 1991	110,000 people
	627,758 people

John Tagliabue, "Young Germans Still Flock to West," *New York Times*, March 11, 1991.

But East Germans were not the only people who came. People with German origin from all over Eastern Europe tried to find entrance into West Germany:

People with German Origin Settled
in West Germany

	Total	Poland	USSR	Romania	Other Countries
1988	202,673	140,321	47,572	12,902	1,878
1989	377,055	250,340	93,134	23,387	10,194
1990	397,073	133,872	147,950	111,150	4,101

"1990 mehr Aussiedler nach Deutschland als jemals zuvor," *Frankfurter Allgemeine Zeitung*, January 4, 1991.

E. The Political Unification of Germany

1. A precise overview of the international political problems surrounding the unification can be found in Karl Kaiser, "Germany's Unification," *Foreign Affairs*, Vol. 70, No. 1, 1990/91, pp. 179–205.

2. Serge Schnemann, "East Germans Form Grand Coalition," *New York Times*, April 10, 1990.

3. Monika Zimmermann, "Die Volkskammer muss muehsam das Sprechen wieder lernen," *Frankfurter Allgemeine Zeitung*, April 14, 1990.

4. Nina Grunenberg, "Ohne Euphorie und Ueberschwang, Wie Helmut Kohl die Chance ergriff," *Die Zeit*, No. 30, July 27, 1990.

5. Robert Leicht, "Vereinigung im freien Fall, Die DDR zerbricht unter der boesen Erblast: Jetzt gilt es Panik zu wehren," *Die Zeit*, No. 26, June 29, 1990.

6. Friedrich Karl Fromme, "Der Wahlrechtspraezeptor, Das Bundesverfassungsgericht hat das Verfahren bei der gesamtdeutschen Wahl zweimal korrigiert," *Frankfurter Allgemeine Zeitung*, October 24, 1990.

7. Peter Christ, "Lust an der Konfrontation, Wie die Ostberliner Parteien die Koalitionsregierung sprengten und sich selbst entmachteten: ein Tagebuch," *Die Zeit*, No. 35, August 31, 1990.

8. Helmut Schmidt, "Deutschlands grosse Chance," *Die Zeit*, No. 41, October 12, 1990.

9. Margit Gerste, "Gerechtigkeit fuer die Frauen, Wir brauchen

eine gesamdeutsche Fristenloesung," *Die Zeit*, No. 37, September 14, 1990.

The conservatives did not succeed in forbidding abortion in East Germany. Now they wanted to make it a crime for a West German woman to go to East Germany to have an abortion. The law clearly states that a crime is only committed when the law of the location is violated. The SPD and the F.D.P. rejected this notion and prevailed. Friedrich Karl Fromme, "In Sachen Paragraph 218 bleibt die DDR weiterhin Rechts–Ausland," *Frankfurter Allgemeine Zeitung*, September 1, 1990.

10. Bananas, Hohenthal, and Broichhausen, "Damit gilt dieses Grundgesetz fuer das gesamte deutsche Volk, Der Einigungsvertrag," *Frankfurter Allgemeine Zeitung*, August 28, 1990.

11. Richard von Weizsaecker, "In einem vereinten Europa dem Frieden der Welt dienen," *Frankfurter Allgemeine Zeitung*, October 4, 1990.

Helmut Kohl, "Die Erfuellung eines geschichtlichen Auftrages," *Frankfurter Allgemeine Zeitung*, October 2/3, 1990.

12. Elisabeth Noelle–Neumann, "Eine grosse Mehrheit in Ost und West befuerwortet die Einheit," *Frankfurter Allgemeine Zeitung*, August 28, 1990.

13. Angela Stent wrote, "The psychological impact of uniting the two Germanies will be conciderably greater than statistics suggest." Angela Stent, "The One Germany," *Foreign Policy*, No. 81, Winter 1990/91, pp. 53–70.

PART IV

A. The State Election in East Germany and the Federal Election in Germany as a Whole

1. *The Economist*, June 2, 1990, p. 51.

2. The Gorbrecht plan, for example, suggested uniting Lower Saxony with the states of Bremen and Hamburg. It was never seriously discussed. Now the suggestion was made to merge some of the East German with the West German states to facilitate the democratization process. A merger of Hesse and Thuringia was suggested. This idea died like all other suggestions because the ethnic differences between the regions were still remarkably strong.

"Laendereinfuehrungsgesetz am 22. Juli in der Volkskammer," *Frankfurter Allgemeine Zeitung*, July 11, 1990.

3. Forschungsgruppe Wahlen, "Alles dreht sich um die Einheit," *Die Zeit*, No. 43, October 26, 1990.

4. Jochen Steinmayr, "Die Sachsen und ihr kleiner Koenig," *Die Zeit*, No. 44, November 2, 1990.

5. The analysis of the election results pointed into the direction of a consolidation of the party system and a decline in sympathy for the communist successor party. Forschungsgruppe Wahlen suggested that the hard–core support group of the PDS declined to 15 percent.

Forschungsgruppe Wahlen, "Alles dreht sich um die Einheit," *Die Zeit*, No. 43, October 26, 1990.

6. "Die offiziellen Wahlergebnisse," *Frankfurter Allgemeine Zeitung*, December 5, 1990.

For purposes of comparison, the results of prior elections are shown:

	The West German Election 1987	The East German Election 3/18/90
CDU/CSU	44.3	48.1
F.D.P.	9.1	5.3
SPD	37.0	21.8
The Greens	8.3	4.9*
PDS	–	16.3

*This is the added result for The Greens and Buendnis 90.

How the German States Voted
(in Percent)

State	CDU	SDP	FDP	The Greens	PDS
States in Former West Germany					
Baden–Wuerttemberg	46.5	20.1	12.3	5.7	0.3
Bavaria	51.9	26.7	8.7	4.6	0.2
Bremen	30.9	42.5	12.8	8.3	1.1
Hamburg	36.6	41.0	12.0	5.8	1.1
Hesse	41.3	38.0	10.9	5.6	0.4
Lower Saxony	44.3	38.4	0.3	4.5	0.3
North Rhine–Westphalia	40.5	41.1	11.0	4.3	0.3

Rhineland–Palatinate	45.6	36.1	10.4	4.0	0.2
Saarland	38.1	51.2	6.0	2.3	0.2

States in Former East Germany

Brandenburg	36.3	32.9	9.7	6.6	11.0
Mecklenburg–Pomerania	41.2	26.6	9.1	5.9	14.2
Saxony	49.5	18.2	12.4	5.9	9.0
Saxony–Anhalt	38.6	24.7	19.7	5.3	9.4
Thuringia	45.2	21.9	14.6	6.1	8.3
Berlin	39.3	30.5	9.5	7.2	9.7

Source: *The New York Times*, December 4, 1990.

7. Elisabeth Noelle–Neumann, "Der Optimismus hat gesiegt," *Frankfurter Allgemeine Zeitung*, December 5, 1990.

8. Gary Geipel, "To Secure Germany, Kohl Must Still Win Youth," *Wall Street Journal*, December 4, 1990.

9. Kurt Reumann, "Die SPD hat keineswegs die Jugend für sich gewonnen," *Frankfurter Allgemeine Zeitung*, December 4, 1990.

10. Peter Siebenmorgen, "Ein Buendnis ohne Alternative," *Die Zeit*, No. 2, January 4, 1990.

11. Werner Maser, *Helmut Kohl, Der Deutsche Kanzler*, (Berlin: Ullstein Verlag, 1990), pp. 272–296.

12. **The Election in Berlin**

December 2, 1990

	Votes	Seats
CDU/CSU	40.3	100
SPD	30.5	76
F.D.P.	7.1	18
The Greens–West	5.0	12
The Greens–East	4.4	11
PDS	9.2	23
Others	3.5	–
	100.0	240

The coalition negotiations ended, as expected, in a grand coalition between the CDU/CSU and the SPD. "Nur eine grosse Koalition ist moeglich," *Frankfurter Allegmeine Zeitung*, December 4, 1990.

B. The Communist Heritage and the Legacy It Left Behind

1. At the beginning of 1989 the communist party had 2.3 million members and 44,000 functionaries. After the downfall of the regime and the election on March 18, 1990, the number of party members had declined to 320,000. Less than 1 percent of the membership joined the party after November 9, 1989, indicating the deterioration of its attractiveness. Manfred Wilke, "Statt der Arbeiterklasse die soziale Bewegungen," *Frankfurter Allgemeine Zeitung*, October 30, 1990.

2. *The Economist* wrote further that "the budget for 1989 would have dazzled most intelligence agencies: 3.6 billion Ostmarks. Even in real money—and remember that at home the Stasi's costs were in Ostmarks—that was a lot: say $1 billion." "The undergrowth of evil," *The Economist*, December 1, 1990, pp. 19–21.

3. On June 17, 1953, East German workers demonstrated in East Berlin against the communist regime. Soviet tanks protected the East German regime and crushed the protests.

Weltgeschichte der Nachkriegszeit, Band 1, 1947–1957 (Wuerzburg: Ploetz AG, 1957), p. 55.

4. Craig R. Whitney, "Severed German Families Starting to Mend," *New York Times*, December 1, 1990.

Christian Wernicke, "Das Ende einer deutschen Karriere, Lothar de Maiziere gibt auf, doch er will Klarheit in der Sache Cerny," *Die Zeit*, No. 52, December 21, 1990.

5. Hans Ruediger Karutz, "Wir werden Euch zeigen, was Demokratie heisst," *Das Jahr der Deutschen Einheit*, ed. Die Welt (Berlin: Ulstein Verlag, 1990), pp. 64–68.

Interview with Egon Krenz, "Fall of Berlin Wall Was More a Comedy of Errors than by Design," *The Sun Diego Union*, November 4, 1990.

6. Hans Juergensen, "Auf einem dritten Weg zum Sozialismus," *Frankfurter Allgemeine Zeitung*, February 1, 1990.

Karl-Heinz Paque, "Die Schimaere aus dem Nirgendwo, Marktwirtschaft und Sozialismus lassen sich nicht zur Mischform einer sozialistischen Marktwirtschaft verschmelzen, Zur Reformdebatte in der DDR," *Frankfurter Allgemeine Zeitung*, January 13, 1990.

7. I visited East Berlin in December, 1990. There I had ample opportunities to talk to people in the streets, office buildings, and hotels. Again and again people complained that their lives had become

harder since unification and that they had exchanged one oppressive government by another.

8. Peter Bender wrote, "The East Germans . . . enjoyed some respect as long as they were citizens of a strong–minded state that knew how to represent its interests. Since these people have left communism and tried to come under the wings of West Germany they are continuously losing respect and political weight. The East Germans gave up their state and now realize that they have put their fate into the hands of an unknown power. . . . The Germans were separated from each other for almost half a century. The gap between them is much wider than they believed possible. . . . Astute observers said early on that this was not a 're–unification' but a 'new–unification' of dissimilar parts. Peter Bender, "Die geeinte Nation–zutiefst geteilt," *Die Zeit*, No. 8, February 22, 1991.

9. Helmut Klages, "Es fehlt die Bereitschaft zum bedingungslosen Aermelaufkrempeln, Enttaeuschte Erwartungen, fehlender Aufschwung in den neuen Laendern," *Frankfurter Allgemeine Zeitung*, February 16, 1991.

10. Fritz Ullrich Fack, "Die alten Seilschaften leben noch," *Frankfurter Allgemeine Zeitung*, October 23, 1990.

11. The study of the Institut der Deutschen Wirtschaft of Cologne documents with many details how former communists tried to favorably position themselves for the democratic era. The study shows three distinct periods:

A. November 1989 to January 1990—the deliberate effort to position the PDS as successor organization for the communist party and the secret service.

B. January 1990 to March 1990—formation of private enterprises with money of the communist party and putting reliable former communists into leading positions.

C. April 1990 to September 1990—networking of former communists into the new administration. Institut der Deutschen Wirtschaft, Koeln, "SED–Leute in Schluesselstellungen," *Frankfurter Allgemeine Zeitung*, November 23, 1990.

Hans Modrow, honorable chairman of the PDS, wrote in the magazine *Neues Deutschland* that, "The depth of the problem was not correctly realized and the party leadership did not entertain the necessary dialogue with the party base." However, one must realize that many party leaders were former communists. A few examples shall underline this claim:

- Rainer Boerner, thirty–four years old, former member of the Volkskammer (parliament) and the first deputy who admitted working for the secret police.

- Professor Uwe–Jens Heuer, former Dean of the Institute for State Theory at the Academy of Science, now deputy chairman of the PDS in the German parliament.

- Professor Klaus Steinitz, fifty–seven years old, former deputy director of the Institute for Economics; now deputy in the Bundestag and head of the PDS commission for party finances.

- Professor Klaus Hoepcke, fifty–seven years old, former deputy minister for culture; now journalist.

- Lothar Bisky, forty–nine years old, former Dean of the University for Movie and Television in Potsdam–Babelsberg.

- Hans–Joachim Willerding, thirty–eight years old, former secretary of the central committee of the FDJ (communist youth organization).

- Guenter Wieland, forty–six years old, former State prosecutor. "Modrow droht mit Ruecktritt," *Frankfurter Allgemeine Zeitung*, November 7, 1990.

12. Detlev Karsten Rohwedder, "Aufgabe von furchterregender Dimension," *Frankfurter Allgemeine Zeitung*, September 14, 1990.

13. *Frankfurter Allgemeine Zeitung*, April 2, 1990, and June 16, 1990.

14. John Tagliabue, "Secret Police Scandals Outlive East Germany," *New York Times*, October 28, 1990.

15. "Der Vorstand der PDS spricht Gysi das Vertrauen aus," *Frankfurter Allgemeine Zeitung*, October 29, 1990.

16. On October 26, 1990, German authorities stopped the illegal transfer of DM 107 million ($69 million) from PDS accounts to the Soviet Union. The PDS member Karl–Heinz Kaufmann and two arrested PDS leaders, Wolfgang Pohl and Wolfgang Langnitschke, admitted that the transfer was made to avoid confiscation of the money and to establish a secret account. Peter Jochen Winters, "Die Ueberweisung der PDS–Millionen war ein klarer Verstoss gegen das Gesetz," *Frankfurter Allgemeine Zeitung*, October 24, 1990.

Interview with party chairman Gysi, "Gysi kuendigt wirklichen Schnitt in der Eigentumsfrage an," *Frankfurter Allgemeine Zei-*

tung, October 30, 1990.

17. Peter Christ, "Begehrte Altlasten, Zug um Zug kommt das versteckte Vermoegen der PDS zum Vorschein," *Die Zeit*, No. 45. November 9, 1990.

18. One of those enterprises was formed out of the party-owned cars. This company was given to the former SED party secretary of Berlin, Albrecht. Robert Leicht argued, "Dictators and their accomplices cannot legally acquire assets and therefore all of the PDS's assets should be confiscated." Robert Leicht, "Hoechste Zeit fuer scharfe Schnitte," *Die Zeit*, No. 45, November 9, 1990.

19. Johann Michael Moeller, "Ein ernster Biedenkopf ruft die alten Bundeslaender zur Unterstuetzung auf," *Frankfurter Allgemeine Zeitung*, November 9, 1990.

20. Angela Stent, "The One Germany," *Foreign Policy*, No. 81, Winter 1990/91, pp. 53-70.

C. The Economic Outlook for East Germany

1. Lutz Hoffmann, "Preise, Politik Und Prioritaeten, Die Oekonomen sind nicht ratlos beim Uebergang von der Planwirtschaft zur Marktwirtschaft, Erfahrungen und Lehren," *Frankfurter Allgemeine Zeitung*, February 2, 1991.

2. Peter Christ, "Rosskur ohne Medizin," *Die Zeit*, No. 33, August 17, 1990.

3. The speed of the decline of industrial production is alarming. In January, 1990 it was 10 percent below the level of the prior year. In July the decline reached 40 percent and in October it was already above 50 percent. Ferdinand Protzman, "Privatization Is Floundering in East Germany," *New York Times*, March 12, 1991.

4. Alexander Schalck-Golodkowski, "Ich habe mich korrekt abgemeldet," *Die Zeit*, No. 3, January 18, 1991.

5. "Der Kanzler ruft zu Initiative und Leistungsbereitschaft auf, In diesem Jahr hundert Milliarden fuer die oestlichen Bundeslaender," *Frankfurter Allgemeine Zeitung*, March 14, 1991.

6. **The Bundespost's Plans for New Phone Lines in East Germany**

1990	–	100,000
1991	–	600,000
1992	–	800,000

1993 – 1,200,000
1994 – 1,400,000
1995 – 1,400,000
1996 – 1,600,000

The outlays for this modernization program are estimated to be DM 55 billion ($35.5 billion). Kathie Hafner, "German Phone System is Taxed by Unification," *New York Times*, December 12, 1990.

7. "Zweieinhalb Milliarden fuer ostdeutschen Strassenbau," *Frankfurter Allgemeine Zeitung*, February 8, 1991.

8. The Secretary of State in the Economic Ministry in Bonn, Otto Schlecht, argued that the present politics lack the convincing and engaging attitude of Luwdig Erhard, the "father of the economic miracle in 1949." Erhard would have requested the permission to assume sole responsibility for the social and economic unification from Chancellor Kohl and immediately after October 3, 1990, would have stunned the public with words and deeds. As a personified optimist and visionary he would have spoken to the East Germans weekly at prime TV time. He would have asked the people to understand that sacrifices would be needed first before their econonic fortunes would get better. But he would have created an atmosphere of confidence and trust that would have made the trying times easier. By October, he would have initiated cash advances for large public investments and he would never have hesitated to ask the West Germans for a solidarity payment in the form of higher temporary taxes, mainly because they had such a large windfall profit from the unification. Finally, he would have cut drastically the outdated subsidies that are such a burden for the federal budget.

"Schlecht: Was Ludwig Erhard getan haette," *Frankfurter Allgemeine Zeitung*, March 27, 1991.

9. The German goverment agreed on a tax increase, including an income tax hike of 7.5 percent for one year, that increases the government's revenue by DM 46 billion ($29.7 billion). This tax increase was needed to provide DM 50 billion ($32.3 billion) in cash for immediate investments in East Germany. "Neue Laender koennen 1991 mehr als 50 Milliarden investieren," *Frankfurter Allgemeine Zeitung*, March 2, 1991.

10. Labor Minister Norbert Bluem argued that given the present competitive situation the following jobs are obsolete:

1,200,000 in the export industry
700,000 in the public administration
400,000 in agriculture
220,000 in mining
550,000 in the electro industry

According to this study, about one–third of the total work force of 8.9 million will be out of work if no new jobs are created. Heinz Bluethmann/Dirk Kurbjuweit, "Ende einer Illusion," *Die Zeit*, No. 8, February 22, 1990.

"Die Beschaeftigung im Osten sinkt weiter," *Frankfurter Allgemine Zeitung*, March 7, 1991.

11. Peter Christ wrote, "After one year of optimistic speeches and half–hearted deeds it finally dawns on the government that the economy of East Germany is on its way to a catastrophe. The Bonn politicians have wasted valuable time because they believed in their own propaganda and not the gloomy but realistic forecasts of the economic profession." Peter Christ, "Erst die Einheit, nun die Pleite, Wenn die Bonner Politiker nicht endlich aufwachen, bricht in Ostdeutschland alles zusammen," *Die Zeit*, No. 8, February 22, 1991.

"Trennendes Geld, Westliche Laender signalisieren mehr Hilfe für Ostdeutschland," *Frankfurter Allgemeine Zeitung*, February 8, 1991.

12. German exports grew by DM 26.7 billion ($17.2 billion) to DM 668 billion ($431 billion) in 1990. Imports grew by DM 51.4 billion ($33.1 billion) tc DM 558 billion ($360 billion). The trade balance shrank by DM 24.7 billion ($15.9 billion) to DM 110 billion ($71 billion). The balance on current accounts declined by DM 30 billion ($19.4 billion) to DM 75.5 billion ($61.2 billion). "Aus dem Bundesbank Bericht, Die deutschen Kapitalausfuhren nehmen ab," *Frankfurter Allgemeine Zeitung*, February 18, 1991, and "Ueberschusee sind zurueckgegangen," *Frankfurter Allgemeine Zeitung*, February 2, 1991.

CONCLUSION

One Final Look Back and a Few Remarks
About the Future

1. Three former French Foreign Minister Jean François Poncet said, "Kohl seized the opportunity of unification with such decisive-

ness that he irritated many of his allies. . . . But he is now emerging as one of the great European leaders of the post–war period, and this was certainly unexpected. He has produced the image of a strong, powerful, and rich Germany that is nevertheless democratic, pro– European, and not dangerous. He hasn't made a single significant mistake." Frederick Kempe, "Helmut Kohl Takes Europe's Center Stage, Surprising His Critics, Award Politician by Nature, He Seized on Unification as a Moment in History," *Wall Street Journal*, November 30, 1990.

2. The *Frankfurter Allgemeine Zeitung* reported: "After the U. S. Great Britain, and France had ratified the two–plus–four agreement, the fourth victorious power starts its parliamentary ratification process now. . . . However, strong forces in the Supreme Soviet want to condition their approval on receiving additional loans and other favors from Germany." "Der Oberste Soviet debattiert ueber die Deutschlandsvertraege," *Frankfurter Allgemeine Zeitung*, February 14, 1991.

3. Fritz Ullrich Fack, "Hilfe, die dringend benoetigt wird," *Frankfurter Allgemeine Zeitung*, February 15, 1991.

4. Helmut Schmidt, "Deutschlands grosse Chance, Einheit in Freiheit: Wir duerfen unser Glueck nicht durch Ueberheblichkeit gefaehrden," *Die Zeit*, No. 41, October 12, 1990.

5. Theo Sommer, "Die Deutschen an die Front?, Anmerkungen zur weltpolitischen Rolle des geeinten Deutschlands am Ende des zwanzigsten Jahrhunderts," *Die Zeit*, No. 13., March 29, 1991.

6. "Kohl: Ich habe mich getaeuscht," *Frankfurter Allgemeine Zeitung*, March 1, 1991.

7. Helmut Klages, "Es fehlt an der Bereitschaft zum bedingungslosem Aermelaufkrempeln, Enttaeuschte Erwartungen, fehlender Aufschwung," *Frankfurter Allgemeine Zeitung*, February, 16, 1991.

8. Detlev Karsten Rohwedder was shot to death through the window of his house in Duesseldorf on the Monday after Easter, April 1, 1991. The Red Army Faction took responsibility for this action in a letter found at the scene. Stephen Kinzer, "Red Army Faction Is Suspected in German Killing," *New York Times*, April 3, 1991.

9. The 1990 economic estimates for Eastern Europe by the U. N. Commission on Europe (ECE):

	Eastern Europe	USSR
Industrial Production	-20 percent	-1.5 percent
GNP	-11 percent	-5.0 percent
Investments in Plants		
and Structures	-20 percent	-12.0 percent

Osteuropa geht durch ein Tal der Rezession," *Frankfurter Allgemeine Zeitung*, November 28, 1990.

*   *   *   *   *

Throughout the essay, the Deutsche Mark is converted into U. S. dollar at the rate of DM 1.55 equals $1.00.

*   *   *   *   *